TRUE STORIES

In the News

A BEGINNING READER

THIRD EDITION

by Sandra Heyer

PEARSON
Longman

To John, first reader of all the True Stories

True Stories in the News, Third Edition

Pearson Education, 10 Bank Street, White Plains, NY 10606

Staff credits: The people who made up the *True Stories in the News, Third Edition* team, representing editorial, production, design, and manufacturing, are Karen Davy, Nancy Flaggman, Robert Ruvo, Barbara Sabella, and Paula Van Ells.

Photo credits: Unit 1—Dish Soap for Dinner (Sandra Heyer); **Unit 2**—A New Man (Wide World Photos); **Unit 3**—The Runner (Carrie Dampier); **Unit 4**—The Love Letters (Sandra Heyer; Fotosearch); **Unit 5**—Bad Luck, Good Luck (Richard Klune/Corbis; Tom Grill/Corbis); **Unit 6**—Lost and Found (Wide World Photos); **Unit 7**—A Little Traveler (Union Tribune Publishing Company); **Unit 8**—Man's Best Friend (Courtesy of VisitBritain.com); **Unit 9**—The Coin (David Cavenagh/*Illawarra Mercury*); **Unit 10**—Love or Baseball? (Jeff Christensen/Reuters; Ray Stubblebine/Reuters/Corbis); **Unit 11**—Buried Alive (Sandra Heyer); **Unit 12**—The Winning Ticket (Cap Carpenter/*San Jose Mercury News*); **Unit 13**—Thank You (Courtesy of Kathi Koontz/The Marine Mammal Center; John Hyde/Wild Things Photography); **Unit 14**—Together Again (Al Diaz/*Miami Herald*); **Unit 15**—Saved by the Bell (Mark Seelen/zefa/Corbis); **Unit 16**—This Is the Place for Me (*Daily Herald*; Stephen M. Carrera/Wide World Photos); **Unit 17**—Nicole's Party (Daily News Pix); **Unit 18**—A Strong Little Boy (Bill Hogan/*Chicago Tribune*); **Unit 19**—The Champion (Courtesy of Hungarian Olympic Committee; IOC/Olympic Museum Collections); **Unit 20**—The Bottle (Dale Wittner); **Unit 21**—The Last Laugh (*News Herald*); **Unit 22**—Old Friends (Courtesy of Chi Hsii Tsui)

Text composition: Integra Software Services
Text font: 11.5/13 New Aster
Illustrations: Don Martinetti

Library of Congress Cataloging-in-Publication Data

True stories in the news / [compiled by] Sandra Heyer. —3rd ed.
   p.   cm.
ISBN 0-13-615481-6 (student bk. w/ audio : alk. paper) 1. English
language—Textbooks for foreign speakers.   2. Current
events—Problems, exercises, etc.   3. Readers—Current events. I.
Heyer, Sandra.
PE1128.H4364 2007
428.6'4—dc22   2007039897

ISBN: 0-13-615481-6

Printed in the United States of America
2 3 4 5 6 7 8 9 10—CRS—11 10 09 08

Contents

Introduction

True Stories in the News is a beginning reader for students of English. It consists of 22 units based on human-interest stories adapted from newspapers and magazines. The vocabulary and structures used in the stories are carefully controlled to match those of a typical beginning ESL class. At the same time, all attempts were made to keep the language natural.

In answer to those students who think some stories are too amazing to be true: Yes, the stories are true, to the best of our knowledge. A special "To the Teacher" section at the back of the book provides additional information about each story.

Following are some suggestions for using *True Stories in the News*. Teachers new to the field might find these suggestions especially helpful. Please remember that these are only suggestions. Teachers should, of course, feel free to adapt these strategies to best suit their teaching styles and their students' learning styles.

PRE-READING

Beneath the photo that introduces each unit are two sets of questions. The first set guides students as they describe the photo. The second set asks students to speculate on the content of the reading.

Each story in Levels 1 and 2 of the *True Stories* series—*Very Easy True Stories, All New Very Easy True Stories, Easy True Stories,* and *All New Easy True Stories*—is introduced with a sequence of drawings. Before students read, the teacher tells them the story while they look at the drawings. This Level 3 book has no pre-reading drawings. However, before students read, you can still tell them the gist of the story while drawing your own illustrations on the board. Only a few simple sketches can have a dramatic effect on subsequent reading comprehension, so this pre-reading activity is well worth the five or ten minutes you devote to it. If you're not skilled at drawing—and many of us are not—please see the drawing tips in the To the Teacher section at the back of the book. Also in the To the Teacher section are many suggestions for pre-, during-, and post-reading activities.

THE EXERCISES

Each unit has four types of exercises: vocabulary, comprehension, discussion, and writing. In some units, there is a pronunciation exercise as well. Students can complete the exercises individually, in pairs, in small groups, or as a whole-class activity. The exercises can be completed in class or assigned as homework. At the back of the book, there is an answer key to the exercises.

VOCABULARY

The vocabulary exercises highlight words that ESL students identified as new and that could be clearly drawn, described, or defined. The exercises clarify meaning while giving students practice in establishing meaning through contextual clues. In the To the Teacher section at the back of the book, there are suggestions for supplemental vocabulary activities.

PRONUNCIATION

This exercise helps students correlate English vowels with the sounds they represent. Students, especially those whose first language is phonetic, are usually surprised to discover that the five English vowels make more than five sounds. The purpose of the exercise is simply to make students aware that these sounds exist in English, not to drill students into pronouncing the sounds perfectly. (In fact, doing so would probably be a disservice.) Keep in mind that some vowels make one sound when they are stressed, as they are in the exercise, but change to the neutral vowel /ə/ when they are in an unstressed position. Consider how the pronunciation of the "a" in "and" changes when "and" is put in an unstressed position: "cream and sugar."

COMPREHENSION

The comprehension exercises test students' understanding of the story; more important, the exercises help students develop reading skills they will use throughout their reading careers—skills such as scanning, summarizing, identifying the main idea, and recognizing connectors and other rhetorical devices.

DISCUSSION

Most of the discussion exercises require students to complete a task—to fill in a chart, to interview a classmate, to draw a picture or a map—so that there is a concrete focus to the discussion. The task-centered exercises make it possible for students to talk without the direct supervision of the teacher, a necessity in large classes.

Several of the discussion exercises ask students to compare their native countries to the United States. Teachers in Canada and Australia can adapt these exercises easily by substituting those countries for the words "the United States." Teachers whose students are learning English in their native countries will need to modify those exercises that draw specifically on the immigrant/foreign student experience. In the To the Teacher section at the back of the book, you will find alternate discussion exercises suitable for students who are learning English in their home countries.

In some units, the discussion activity and the writing activity are based on a single task. In those units, the discussion and writing exercises are blended into a single two-part exercise section labeled Discussion/Writing (or sometimes Writing/Discussion).

WRITING

Most of the writing exercises are structured: Students complete sentences, answer questions, and create lists. Students who are fairly accomplished writers may need more challenging assignments, such as writing short paragraphs. Students who are less experienced writers may need to see some sample responses before they write.

The vocabulary, comprehension, discussion, and writing exercises are at approximately parallel levels; that is, they assume that students speak and write about as well as they read. Of course, that is not always the case. Please feel free to tamper with the exercises—to adjust them up or down to suit students' proficiency levels, to skip some, or to add some of your own.

Both the exercises and reading selections are intended to build students' confidence along with their reading skills. Above all, it is hoped that reading *True Stories in the News* will be a pleasure, for both you and your students.

UNIT 1

1. PRE-READING

Look at the picture.

▸ What is the man putting on his salad?

▸ Why do you think he is doing that?

Read the title of the story. Look at the picture again.

▸ What do you think this story is about?

▸ Can you guess what happens?

Dish Soap for Dinner

Joe came home from work and opened his mailbox. In his mailbox, he found a yellow bottle of soap—soap for washing dishes.

The dish soap was a free sample from a soap company. The company mailed small bottles of soap to millions of people. It was a new soap with a little lemon juice in it. The company wanted people to try it.

Joe looked at his free bottle of soap. There was a picture of two lemons on the label. Over the lemons were the words "with Real Lemon Juice."

"Good!" Joe thought. "A free sample of lemon juice! I'm going to have a salad for dinner. This lemon juice will taste good on my salad." Joe put the soap on his salad and ate it. After Joe ate the salad, he felt sick.

Joe wasn't the only person who got sick. A lot of people thought the soap was lemon juice. They put the soap on fish, on salads, and in tea. Later they felt sick, too. Some people had stomachaches but felt better in a few hours. Some people felt really sick and went to the hospital. Luckily, no one died from eating the soap.

What can we learn from Joe's story? Read labels carefully. And don't eat dish soap for dinner!

2. VOCABULARY

Complete the sentences. Find the right words. Circle the letter of your answer.

1. The dish soap was a _____ from a soap company.
   a. letter
   b. free sample
   c. mailbox

2. The company wanted people to _____ the soap.
   a. try
   b. eat
   c. mail

3. There was a picture of two lemons on the _____.
   a. soap company
   b. label
   c. salad

4. What can we learn from Joe's story? Read labels _____.
   a. fast
   b. happily
   c. carefully

3. COMPREHENSION

◆ REMEMBERING DETAILS

One word in each sentence is not correct. Find the word and cross it out. Write the correct word.

1. In his mailbox, Joe found a ~~green~~ *yellow* bottle of soap.

2. The dish soap was a free ticket from a soap company.

3. It was a new soap with a little orange juice in it.

4. The company wanted people to eat it.

5. There was a picture of two bananas on the label.

6. Joe put the soap on his dishes.

7. After he ate the salad, Joe felt fine.

8. A lot of people thought the soup was lemon juice.

9. They put the soap on fish, on salads, and in coffee.

◆ UNDERSTANDING CAUSE AND EFFECT

Find the best way to complete each sentence. Write the letter of your answer on the line.

1. The company mailed soap to people _d_

2. There was a picture of two lemons on the label ____

3. Joe put the soap on his salad ____

4. Some people went to the hospital ____

a. because they ate the soap and got sick.

b. because he thought the soap was lemon juice.

c. because the soap had a little lemon juice in it.

d. because it wanted people to try the soap.

◆ UNDERSTANDING A SUMMARY

Imagine this: You want to tell the story "Dish Soap for Dinner" to a friend. You want to tell the story quickly, in only two sentences. Which two sentences tell the story best? Check (✓) your answer.

☐ 1. Joe came home from work and opened his mailbox. He was happy because he found a free sample—a yellow bottle of dish soap.

☐ 2. A soap company mailed soap to millions of people. Some people thought the soap was lemon juice, so they ate it and got sick.

4. DISCUSSION

Joe made a mistake: He put dish soap on his salad. Do you have a story about a mistake you made? Did you make a mistake when you

- traveled by plane, bus, train, or subway?
- bought food?
- ordered food in a restaurant?
- used a computer?
- used a phone?
- went to school?
- went to work?

On the lines below, write a few sentences about your experience. Then share your sentences with a partner. Here, for example, is what one student wrote.

I made a mistake when I traveled by subway. I wanted to go to the library, but I went to a town called Library.

_____

_____

_____

5. WRITING

Read this story. It is in the present tense. On your own paper, write the story again in the past tense.

Joe comes home from work and opens his mailbox. In his mailbox, he finds a free sample of dish soap. The dish soap has a little lemon juice in it.

Joe looks at his bottle of soap. There is a picture of two lemons on the label. Over the lemons are the words "with Real Lemon Juice."

Joe thinks the soap is lemon juice. He puts it on his salad and eats it. After he eats the salad, he feels sick. Poor Joe!

Joe came home from work and opened his mailbox.

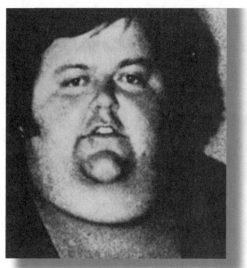

UNIT 2

1. PRE-READING

Look at the pictures.

▶ Do they show two different men or the same man?

▶ What are the man and woman doing?

Read the title of the story. Look at the pictures again.

▶ What do you think this story is about?

▶ Can you guess what happens?

A New Man

The man in the first picture lives in Northern Ireland. His name is Roley McIntyre. Roley McIntyre was big—he was very big. He weighed 600 pounds.[1]

For lunch Roley ate ten pieces of bacon, four eggs, ten potatoes, and fried vegetables. For dinner he ate meat and more potatoes, and after dinner he always ate dessert. Before he went to bed, he ate a few sandwiches and some cake.

Roley couldn't drive a regular car because he was too big. He couldn't fit in the front seat. Roley had a special car. It had no front seat. Roley drove his car from the back seat.

One day Roley went to the doctor. The doctor said, "Mr. McIntyre, you have a special car. Now you need to buy a special coffin—a coffin for a very big man. You have to lose weight, or you're going to die soon."

Roley went on a diet. For breakfast he ate cereal with nonfat milk. For lunch he ate baked beans on toast. For dinner he ate fish and vegetables.

After Roley began to lose weight, he met a pretty woman. Her name was Josephine. Josephine told Roley, "Don't stop your diet."

Roley didn't stop his diet. He continued to lose weight. In 18 months, he lost 400 pounds.[2]

Two years after Roley started his diet, he and Josephine got married. You can see them together in the second picture. Roley and Josephine are wearing a pair of Roley's old pants.

[1] 272 kilograms
[2] 181 kilograms

2. VOCABULARY

Complete the sentences. Find the right words. Circle the letter of your answer.

1. After dinner Roley ate cake, cookies, or ice cream. He always ate _____.
   a. lunch
   b. dessert
   c. breakfast

2. Roley couldn't drive a regular car because he was too big. He couldn't _____ in the front seat.
   a. fit
   b. stand
   c. see

3. The doctor told Roley, "You have a special car. Now you need to buy a special _____ because you're going to die soon."
   a. refrigerator
   b. garage
   c. coffin

4. The doctor told Roley, "You are too big. You have to go on a diet. Don't eat potatoes and dessert. You need to _____."
   a. eat more
   b. lose weight
   c. buy clothes

3. COMPREHENSION

◆ LOOKING FOR DETAILS

What did Roley eat when he was big? Find the words in the story. Write them here.

bacon

eggs

_____

_____

_____

_____

_____

What did Roley eat when he was on a diet? Find the words in the story. Write them here.

cereal with nonfat milk

_____

_____

_____

◆ REVIEWING THE STORY

Complete each sentence. Then read the story again and check your answers.

Roley McIntyre was very big. He _____weighed_____ 600 pounds. Roley
                                        1.
couldn't drive a regular car. He couldn't fit in the front _____,
                                                                     2.
so Roley's car had no front seat. He could drive his car from the

_____ seat.
       3.

Roley's doctor said, "Mr. McIntyre, you have to lose weight, or you're going to

_____ soon." Roley went on a _____. He began
       4.   **5.**
to lose _____. He met a pretty _____.
              6.   **7.**
She told Roley, "Don't _____ your diet." Roley didn't stop
                             8.
his diet; he lost 400 _____.
                            9.

Two years after Roley started his diet, Roley and Josephine got

_____.
       10.

♦ **UNDERSTANDING CAUSE AND EFFECT**

Find the best way to complete each sentence. Write the letter of your answer on the line.

1. Roley McIntyre was big ___c___

2. Roley couldn't drive a regular car ____

3. Roley needed to buy a coffin ____

4. Roley ate only fish and vegetables for dinner ____

5. Roley and Josephine could wear a pair of Roley's old pants ____

a. because he was going to die.

b. because he was on a diet.

c. because he ate a lot.

d. because he couldn't fit in the front seat.

e. because the pants were very big.

4. WRITING/DISCUSSION

What did you usually eat for breakfast, lunch, dinner, and snacks in your native country? What do you usually eat in the United States?

A. Complete the chart.

	IN MY NATIVE COUNTRY, I USUALLY ATE	IN THE UNITED STATES, I USUALLY EAT
Breakfast		
Lunch		
Dinner		
Snacks		

B. Take turns reading your chart to a partner.

▸ Do you and your partner eat the same food?

▸ Which food do you think is healthier—the food you ate in your native country or the food you eat in the United States?

1. PRE-READING

Look at the picture.

▸ What is the woman doing?

▸ How old do you think she is?

Read the title of the story. Look at the picture again.

▸ What do you think this story is about?

▸ Can you guess what happens?

The Runner

One morning a man was driving to work when he saw something unusual: An old woman was running along the street. The man called the police on his cell phone. "I saw a very old woman on Torggate Street," he said. "She was running. Maybe she escaped from a nursing home. Please try to find her."

Two police officers drove to Torggate Street. An old woman was running along the street. The man was right: She was very old—maybe 80 or 90. The police officers stopped their car and ran after the woman.

"Ma'am, please stop!" they said.

The old woman stopped and turned around.

"Are you OK?" the police officers asked.

"Yes, I'm fine," the woman said.

"What's your name, please?" the police officers asked.

"Sigrid Krohn," the woman answered.

"Mrs. Krohn, do you live near here?"

"About a kilometer away," she answered. Mrs. Krohn gave the officers her address.

One of the police officers wrote down the address, walked back to his car, and called the police station. A few minutes later, he returned.

"It's all correct," he told the other police officer. "She lives in her own home, about a kilometer from here."

"Of course, it's correct," Mrs. Krohn said. "There's nothing wrong with my head." Then she patted her legs and smiled. "And there's nothing wrong with my legs."

"Do you mind telling us how old you are?" the police officers asked.

"No, I don't mind," the woman said. "I'm 94."

"You're 94?" the police officers asked.

"That's correct," Mrs. Krohn answered.

"One more question," the police officers said. "Do you mind telling us why you're running?"

Mrs. Krohn looked surprised. "I'm running for exercise," she answered. "Twice a week, I run a kilometer or two. Is it OK if I continue?"

"Of course. Go ahead," the police officers said. "We're sorry we bothered you."

"No problem," Mrs. Krohn said, and she ran away on her old, strong legs.

2. VOCABULARY

Which words have the same meaning as the words in *italics*? Write the letter of your answer on the line.

___b___ **1.** The man thought, "Maybe the old woman *ran away* from a nursing home."

_____ **2.** Mrs. Krohn's house was only a kilometer away. It was *not far from* Torggate Street.

_____ **3.** The police officer *went back* to his car.

_____ **4.** Mrs. Krohn said, "There's *no problem* with my head."

_____ **5.** The police officer asked Mrs. Krohn, "Do you mind telling us how old you are?" She answered, "No, *it's OK*."

a. nothing wrong

b. escaped

c. returned

d. I don't mind.

e. near

3. PRACTICING PRONUNCIATION

The underlined words are in the story. If you can say them correctly, you can say the words below them correctly, too. Practice with your teacher.

<u>call</u>	<u>old</u>	<u>man</u>	<u>right</u>	<u>pat</u>
ball	cold	can	fight	cat
fall	hold	pan	light	hat
hall	sold	ran	night	rat
tall	told	van	tight	sat

4. COMPREHENSION

◆ **REMEMBERING DETAILS**

Complete the sentences. Write your answer on the line.

1. The old woman was walking, right?

   No, she wasn't. She was _____*running*_____.

2. The man thought, "Maybe she escaped from a prison," right?

   No, he didn't. He thought, "Maybe she escaped from a

   _____."

3. Two paramedics drove to Torggate Street, right?

   No, two _____.

4. The woman lived about three kilometers away, right?

   No, she didn't. She lived about _____.

5. She gave the police officers her telephone number, right?

   No, she didn't. She gave them her _____.

6. She was 84 years old, right?

   No, she wasn't. She was _____.

◆ **UNDERSTANDING DIALOG**

Match the questions and the answers. Write the letter of your answer on the line. Then practice the conversation with a partner. One student reads the questions, and the other student reads the answers.

_c_ **1.** "Are you OK?"

____ **2.** "What's your name, please?"

____ **3.** "Do you live near here?"

____ **4.** "How old are you?"

____ **5.** "Why are you running?"

a. "I'm 94."

b. "Yes, about a kilometer away."

c. "Yes, I'm fine."

d. "I'm running for exercise."

e. "Mrs. Krohn."

5. WRITING/DISCUSSION

A. Mrs. Krohn was 94 years old. Think about an old person you know and like. Complete the sentences.

1. I am thinking about _____.

2. He/She is _____ years old.

3. He/She lives in _____.

4. Every day he/she _____.

5. When he/she was young, he/she _____.

6. I like him/her because _____.

B. Read the sentences you wrote above to a partner. Tell your partner a little more about the person.

UNIT
4

1. PRE-READING

Look at the picture.

▶ What do you see in the picture?

▶ In what language is the letter?

Read the title of the story. Look at the picture again.

▶ What do you think this story is about?

▶ Can you guess what happens?

The Love Letters

Ming-fu and Lee met at a party. For Ming-fu, it was love at first sight. "Hello," he said to Lee. "I'm Ming-fu." Lee looked at him and smiled. "Hi," she said. "I'm Lee." Ming-fu and Lee laughed and talked all evening. When they left the party, it was 2 A.M.

For the next year, Ming-fu and Lee were together every weekend. They went everywhere together—to movies, to parks, to museums, and to restaurants.

One night, at a romantic restaurant, Ming-fu asked Lee, "Will you marry me?" "No," Lee answered. "I'm not ready to get married."

"I can't believe it!" Ming-fu thought. "Lee doesn't want to marry me! But I love her! What can I do?" Ming-fu began writing love letters to Lee. Every day he wrote a letter and mailed it to her. "I love you," he said in his letters. "Marry me."

Every day the same mail carrier delivered Ming-fu's letter to Lee. The mail carrier always smiled when he gave Lee a letter. "Another letter from your boyfriend," he said.

Ming-fu sent Lee a love letter every day for two years—700 letters altogether. Finally Lee said, "I'm ready to get married now."

Did Lee marry Ming-fu? No, she didn't. She married the mail carrier who delivered Ming-fu's letters.

2. VOCABULARY

Complete the sentences with the words below.

can't believe it	delivered	love at first sight	ready

1. When Ming-fu met Lee, he loved her immediately. It was _love at first sight_.

2. Lee told Ming-fu, "I don't want to get married now. It's not a good time for me. I'm not _____ to get married now."

3. When Lee told Ming-fu, "I'm not ready to get married," Ming-fu was very surprised. "This is not possible!" he thought. "I _____!"

4. Every day the same mail carrier took Ming-fu's letter to Lee's house. Then he gave the letter to Lee. He _____ Ming-fu's letter.

3. COMPREHENSION

◆ UNDERSTANDING WORD GROUPS

Read each group of words. One word in each group doesn't belong. Find the word and cross it out.

smile	parks	marry	mail carrier
~~run~~	museums	romantic	doctor
laugh	labels	love	letters
talk	restaurants	soccer	send

◆ REMEMBERING DETAILS

One word in each sentence is not correct. Find the word and cross it out. Write the correct word.

1. Ming-fu and Lee met at a ~~concert~~. *party*

2. When they left the party, it was 2 P.M.

3. For the next year, Ming-fu and Lee were together every morning.

4. They went everywhere together—to movies, to parks, to museums, and to schools.

5. One night, at a romantic restaurant, Ming-fu asked Lee, "Will you write me?"

6. Ming-fu began writing postcards to Lee.

7. Ming-fu sent Lee a love letter every day—70 letters altogether.

8. Lee married the mail carrier who wrote Ming-fu's letters.

◆ UNDERSTANDING QUOTATIONS

Find the best way to complete each sentence. Write the letter of your answer on the line.

1. When Ming-fu met Lee, he said, __c__

2. When Ming-fu asked Lee, "Will you marry me?" she said, ____

3. When Ming-fu wrote love letters to Lee, he told her, ____

4. When the mail carrier delivered Ming-fu's letters, he smiled and said, ____

a. "Another letter from your boyfriend."

b. "I love you. Marry me."

c. "Hello. I'm Ming-fu."

d. "No. I'm not ready to get married."

4. DISCUSSION

1. Do you believe in love at first sight? Raise your hands and vote. How many students think love at first sight is possible? How many think it's not possible?

2. When Lee told Ming-fu, "I'm not ready to get married," Ming-fu thought, "What can I do?"

What *can* Ming-fu do? Give him some ideas. First, read the list below with the help of your dictionary or your teacher. Choose the five best ideas. Check (✓) them. Your teacher will read the ideas one by one. First, the women will vote. They will raise their hands for the ideas they checked. Then the men will vote. They will raise their hands for the ideas they checked. Did the men and women choose the same ideas?

Ming-fu wants Lee to marry him. What can he do? He can . . .

☐   1. write love letters to her.
☐   2. call her on the phone every day.
☐   3. sing to her.
☐   4. buy her presents (flowers, candy, jewelry).
☐   5. take her to restaurants for dinner.
☐   6. cook for her.
☐   7. take her dancing.
☐   8. wear nice clothes.
☐   9. be clean and smell good.
☐ 10. listen to her when she talks.
☐ 11. always tell her the truth. Never lie to her.
☐ 12. remember important days—her birthday, for example.
☐ 13. be polite; say "please" and "thank you."
☐ 14. tell her she is beautiful.
☐ 15. be faithful to her. (No other girlfriends!)
☐ 16. _____

(Write your own idea.)

5. WRITING

What do people write in a love letter? Make a list of possible sentences with your classmates. Your teacher will write your sentences on the board.

Ming-fu and Lee lived in Taiwan, so Ming-fu wrote his letters in Chinese. On your own paper, write a love letter from Ming-fu to Lee in English. (You can use the sentences on the board.)

UNIT 5

1. PRE-READING

Look at the picture on the left.

▶ What is the problem with the car?

▶ How do you think it happened?

Look at the picture on the right.

▶ What is in the box?

▶ What is the man's job?

Read the title of the story. Look at the pictures again.

▶ What do you think this story is about?

▶ Can you guess what happens?

Bad Luck, Good Luck

Vegard Olsen is 24 years old. He lives alone, but he visits his parents often. On a Saturday evening, Vegard went to his parents' house for dinner. After dinner, he went to his car to drive home. "Oh, no!" he thought when he saw his car. "My car window is broken! Maybe someone broke into my car!"

Vegard got in the car and looked under the front seat. He usually kept his wallet there. His wallet was gone. In his wallet were some cash, his driver's license, and his credit card. All his music CDs were gone, too. Vegard called the police. Then he called his credit card company. "My credit card was stolen," he told the company.

That night Vegard drove home without his music CDs. It was a quiet ride home.

Vegard works at a pizza restaurant. On Monday he delivered a pizza and some soft drinks to a house near the restaurant. A young man answered the door.

"How much is it?" the man asked Vegard.

"$22.89," Vegard answered.

"Can I pay with a credit card?" the man asked.

"Sure," Vegard said.

The man gave Vegard a credit card. It was Vegard's card! Vegard wanted to say, "Hey! This is my card! Give me my wallet and my music CDs!" But he didn't. He said, "Enjoy your pizza. Have a nice evening." Then he went back to the restaurant and called the police.

The police went to the man's house. Inside they found Vegard's wallet. The cash was gone, but his driver's license and credit card were in the wallet. The police found Vegard's music CDs in the house, too. They gave Vegard all his things back.

That night Vegard drove home from work with his music CDs in his car. He listened to the CDs and sang along with the music. He smiled all the way home.

2. VOCABULARY

Complete the sentences with the words below.

broke into	stolen	wallet	without

1. Vegard's money, driver's license, and credit card were in his _____*wallet*_____.

2. Someone broke a car window and took things from Vegard's car. Vegard called the police and said, "Someone _____ my car."

3. Someone took Vegard's credit card. Vegard called the credit card company and said, "My card was _____."

4. Someone took Vegard's music CDs, so he drove home _____ them.

3. PRACTICING PRONUNCIATION

The underlined words are in the story. If you can say them correctly, you can say the words below them correctly, too. Practice with your teacher.

car	cash	back	found	thing	can
bar	cab	black	ground	king	Dan
far	cap	crack	pound	ring	fan
jar	cat	pack	round	sing	man
star	catch	sack	sound	spring	tan

4. COMPREHENSION

◆ UNDERSTANDING THE MAIN IDEAS

Circle the letter of the correct answer.

1. When Vegard saw the broken car window, he said, "Oh, no!" because
   a. it is expensive to fix a broken window.
   b. he thought, "Maybe someone broke into my car."

2. Vegard looked under the seat because
   a. he usually kept his wallet there.
   b. he usually kept his car keys there.

3. He called his credit card company because
   a. he wanted more credit.
   b. his card was stolen.

4. It was a quiet ride home because
   a. there were no cars on the streets.
   b. Vegard didn't have his music CDs.

5. Two days later, Vegard smiled all the way home because
   a. he had his wallet and CDs back.
   b. he liked to work at the pizza restaurant.

◆ REMEMBERING DETAILS

Read the summary of the story "Bad Luck, Good Luck." There are nine mistakes in the summary. Find the mistakes and cross them out. Write the correct words. (The first one is done for you.)

Vegard Olsen visited his parents on a Saturday ~~morning~~ *evening*. Then he went to

his truck to drive home. A car window was dirty. "Maybe someone broke

into my car!" he thought.

Vegard got in the car and looked under the back seat. His purse was gone.

All his movie CDs were gone, too.

Vegard works at a hamburger restaurant. On Wednesday, he delivered a pizza to a house near the restaurant. A woman paid for the pizza with Vegard's credit card. Vegard called the police.

The police went to the house. They found Vegard's things and gave them back to him.

5. DISCUSSION

A. Someone broke into Vegard's car and took his wallet and CDs. That was a crime. Read the list of crimes below. Check (✓) the crimes that sometimes happen in your native city.

☐ break into a car
☐ take a wallet or purse
☐ hit someone and then take his or her money
☐ go into someone's house and take things
☐ take things from a store
☐ go into a store or bank and take money

☐ take a car
☐ drive while drunk
☐ write with paint on buildings
☐ sell drugs
☐ kill someone
☐ _____

_____
(other)

B. Read the crimes you checked to a partner from another city.

▸ Did you and your partner check the same crimes?

▸ What is the punishment for those crimes in your native country?

▸ Do you have any experience with crime? For example, did someone take your wallet? Tell your partner about it.

▸ What can you do so crimes don't happen to you?

6. WRITING

Write a sentence about the story. The sentence can be true, or it can be false. For example:

Vegard Olsen works at a pizza restaurant. (true)
He lives with his parents. (false)

Copy your sentence on the board. Your classmates will read the sentence and say if it is true or false.

1. PRE-READING

Look at the picture.

▶ Who are these people?

▶ Can you guess how they feel?

Read the title of the story. Look at the picture again.

▶ What do you think this story is about?

▶ Can you guess what happens?

Lost and Found

Bob Shafran was happy. He was at a new school, and the other students were friendly. "Hi, Bob!" they said. But some students said, "Hi, Eddy!" Bob didn't understand. He asked another student, "Why do some students call me Eddy?"

"Oh, that's easy to explain," the student said. "Eddy Galland was a student here last year. Now he goes to a different school. You look like Eddy. Some students think that you're Eddy."

Bob wanted to meet Eddy Galland. He got Eddy's address from a student and went to Eddy's house. Eddy opened the door. Bob couldn't believe his eyes. He looked exactly like Eddy! Bob and Eddy had the same color eyes and the same smile. They had the same dark, curly hair. They also had the same birthday. And they both were adopted.

Bob and Eddy found out that they were twin brothers. Soon after the boys were born, one family adopted Bob, and another family adopted Eddy. Bob's family never knew about Eddy, and Eddy's family never knew about Bob.

Bob and Eddy's story was in the newspaper. There was a photo of Bob and Eddy next to the story. A young man named David Kellman saw the photo in the newspaper. David couldn't believe his eyes. He looked exactly like Bob and Eddy! He had the same color eyes and the same smile. He had the same dark, curly hair. He had the same birthday. And he, too, was adopted.

Later David met Bob and Eddy. When Bob and Eddy saw David, they couldn't believe their eyes. David looked exactly like them! Why did David look exactly like Bob and Eddy? You can probably guess. Bob and Eddy were not twins. Bob, Eddy, and David were triplets.

2. VOCABULARY

Complete the sentences with the words below.

adopted	call	exactly	found out

1. Some students said, "Hi, Eddy!" Bob told another student, "That's not my name. Why do some students _____*call*_____ me Eddy?"

2. Soon after Bob was born, the Shafran family _____ him. He had a new mother and father and a new family.

3. Bob didn't know about Eddy, and Eddy didn't know about Bob. But later they learned that they were brothers. They _____ that they were twin brothers.

4. Bob, Eddy, and David had the same eyes, the same smile, and the same hair. Everything was the same. David looked _____ like Bob and Eddy.

23

3. COMPREHENSION

◆ UNDERSTANDING THE MAIN IDEA

Circle the letter of the best answer.

1. What was "lost and found"?
   a. students
   b. brothers
   c. parents

2. Bob, Eddy, and David were brothers. They didn't know that. Why?
   a. They didn't have the same last name.
   b. They didn't look alike: They had different smiles and noses.
   c. Their parents didn't tell them because they didn't know.

◆ LOOKING FOR DETAILS

Find four correct ways to complete the sentence. Check (✓) your answers.

Bob, Eddy, and David had the same . . .

☐ color eyes.   ☐ dark, curly hair.
☐ smile.   ☐ birthday.
☐ last name.   ☐ address.

◆ UNDERSTANDING CAUSE AND EFFECT

Find the best way to complete each sentence. Write the letter of your answer on the line.

1. Bob Shafran was happy at his new school __e__

2. Bob never saw Eddy at school ____

3. Some students called Bob "Eddy" ____

4. Bob Shafran didn't know he had a brother ____

5. David looked exactly like Bob and Eddy ____

a. because Eddy went to a different school.

b. because Bob looked like Eddy Galland.

c. because his family never knew about Eddy.

d. because Bob, Eddy, and David were triplets.

e. because the other students were friendly.

4. DISCUSSION/WRITING

David looked like Bob and Eddy. What about you? Do you look like anyone in your family?

A. Think about someone in your family—your brother, sister, cousin, mother, father, or child. Who are you thinking of?

Write his or her name here: _____

How are you the same? Check (✓) the words that describe you and the person in your family.

WE HAVE THE SAME . . .	*WE BOTH HAVE . . .*	*WE ARE BOTH . . .*
☐ color eyes.	☐ curly hair.	☐ tall.
☐ color hair.	☐ straight hair.	☐ short.
☐ color skin.	☐ big eyes.	☐ average height.
☐ smile.	☐ big feet.	☐ thin.
☐ teeth.	☐ small feet.	☐ a little heavy.
☐ nose.	☐ big hands.	☐ average weight.
☐ eyebrows.	☐ glasses.	☐ strong.

Read the words you checked to a partner. Tell your partner a little more about the person in your family.

B. Use the information above to write a paragraph. For example, you can begin:

Lina and I are sisters. We have the same color eyes and hair.

_____

_____

_____

_____

_____

_____

_____

UNIT
7

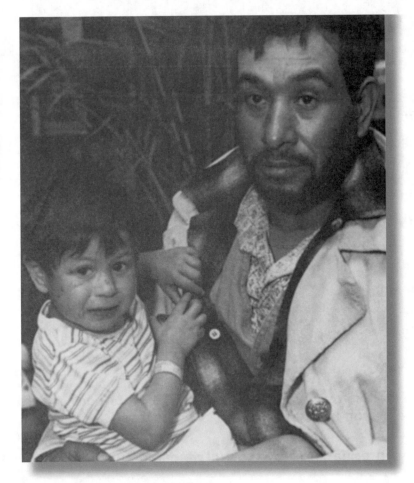

1. PRE-READING

Look at the picture.

▶ Where are these people from?

▶ What kind of work does the man do?

▶ Who is the little boy? How old is he?

Read the title of the story. Look at the picture again.

▶ What do you think this story is about?

▶ Can you guess what happens?

A Little Traveler

Vicente Cabrera is a Mexican farmer. He works in the fields every day. His son, Tomás, is three years old. Tomás often goes to the fields with his father. Mr. Cabrera works, and Tomás plays.

One day Mr. Cabrera went to a field with Tomás. Tomás sat on a rock while Mr. Cabrera worked. Mr. Cabrera looked up from his work. Tomás wasn't on the rock. Mr. Cabrera looked in the field for Tomás. Tomás wasn't there. Mr. Cabrera ran to his house and looked for Tomás. Tomás wasn't there. Mr. Cabrera looked everywhere for Tomás. He couldn't find him.

The Cabrera farm is close to the border between Mexico and the United States. There is a fence at the border, but there are holes in the fence. "Maybe Tomás crawled through a hole in the fence," Mr. Cabrera thought. "Maybe Tomás is in the United States."

The Mexican police telephoned the U.S. Border Patrol. "We need your help," they said. The Mexican police told the U.S. Border Patrol officers about Tomás.

The U.S. Border Patrol officers began to look for Tomás in the United States. They were worried. The land near the border is desert. It is hot in the daytime and cold at night. A small boy can't live long in the desert.

Tomás disappeared on Friday afternoon. On Saturday night, a U.S. Border Patrol officer saw small footprints in the sand. He followed the footprints to a bush. Under the bush, he found Tomás. Tomás was cold, hungry, and thirsty. He had cuts on his feet and face. But he was alive. He was 15 miles[1] from his home.

[1] 24 kilometers

2. VOCABULARY

Complete the sentences. Find the right words. Circle the letter of your answer.

1. The Cabrera farm is close to the border between Mexico and the United States. A _____ is at the border. It separates the United States from Mexico.
   a. restaurant
   b. museum
   c. fence

2. But there are _____ in the fence, and a small boy can crawl through them.
   a. fields
   b. rocks
   c. holes

3. Tomás _____ on Friday afternoon. A U.S. Border Patrol officer found Tomás on Saturday night.
   a. disappeared
   b. worked
   c. changed

4. Tomás walked in the desert for 15 miles. A U.S. Border Patrol officer found his small _____ in the sand.
   a. toys
   b. footprints
   c. shoes

3. COMPREHENSION

◆ FINDING INFORMATION

Read the questions. Find the answers in the story. Write the answers.

1. Is Vicente Cabrera a teacher or a farmer?

   Vicente Cabrera is a farmer.

2. Is his farm in the United States or in Mexico?

   _____

3. Is his farm close to the border or far from the border?

   _____

4. Did Tomás go to the United States or to Mexico?

   _____

5. Did a U.S. Border Patrol officer find Tomás under a bush or under the sand?

   _____

6. Was Tomás dead or alive?

   _____

7. Was Tomás two miles or fifteen miles from his home?

   _____

◆ UNDERSTANDING PRONOUNS

Look at the pronouns. What do they mean? Write the letter of your answer on the line.

_c_ 1. Tomás was sitting on *it*.

____ 2. Tomás crawled through *it*.

____ 3. The Mexican police telephoned *them*.

____ 4. *It* is hot in the daytime and cold at night.

____ 5. A U.S. Border Patrol officer saw *them* in the sand.

____ 6. The officer found Tomás under *it*.

a. footprints

b. the desert

c. a rock

d. a bush

e. the U.S. Border Patrol

f. a hole in the fence

Imagine this: You want to tell the story "A Little Traveler" to a friend. You want to tell the story quickly, in only three sentences. Which three sentences tell the story best? Check (✓) your answer.

☐ **1.** Tomás, a three-year-old Mexican boy, lives close to the border between Mexico and the United States. One day he walked to the border and crawled through a hole in the fence. U.S. Border Patrol officers found him in the United States, 15 miles from his home.

☐ **2.** One day Vicente Cabrera, a Mexican farmer, was working in the fields while his son, Tomás, played on a rock. When Mr. Cabrera looked up from his work, Tomás was gone. Mr. Cabrera looked everywhere for Tomás, but he couldn't find him.

4. DISCUSSION

The United States and Mexico are neighbors. What about your native country?

▸ Does it have neighbors?

▸ Is there a fence at the border?

▸ Is it easy to cross the border?

On your own paper, draw a map of your native country. What are your country's neighbors? Write the names near the borders. Then show your map to a partner. Tell your partner about your native country's neighbors and borders.

5. WRITING

Were you lost when you were a child? Was someone you know lost?

A. First, read about Tomás. Then, on your own paper, write about yourself. (Or write about someone you know.)

1. Tomás was three years old when he was lost. How old were you?

2. Tomás was with his father. Who were you with?

3. Tomás was in a field. Where were you?

4. Tomás walked to the United States. Where did you go?

5. The U.S. Border Patrol found Tomás. Who found you?

6. Tomás was lost for one day. How long were you lost?

B. Read your sentences to a partner. Tell your partner a little more about your experience.

UNIT 8

1. PRE-READING

Look at the picture.

▶ Where is this house?

▶ How old is it?

▶ Can you guess who lived there?

Read the title of the story. Look at the picture again.

▶ What do you think this story is about?

▶ Can you guess what happens?

Man's Best Friend

A long time ago, in a small house in Scotland, two friends lived together. Their names were John and Bobby.

John and Bobby were not rich, but they were happy. They had a warm fire when it was cold outside. They had good food to eat when they were hungry. They were never lonely because they had each other.

John and Bobby liked to take long walks together. After their walk, John usually cooked dinner. John and Bobby ate dinner and then sat in front of the fire. They had a simple but good life.

Then, in the spring of 1858, John got sick and died. He was buried in a cemetery in Edinburgh, Scotland. After John was buried, Bobby stood at John's grave and cried. "Come on, Bobby," friends said. "It's time to go home." Bobby went home, but later he returned to the cemetery. He sat down near John's grave. He stayed there all night.

Bobby stayed at the cemetery the next day, and the next day, and the next. For the next 14 years, Bobby never left the cemetery. When the weather was cold or rainy, he slept in a small house at the cemetery. When the weather was warm, he slept on the ground near John's grave.

Finally, in 1872, Bobby died, too. Friends buried him in a little grave near John. Why was Bobby's grave little? Bobby, John's best friend, was a dog.

2. VOCABULARY

Complete the sentences with the words below.

grave	ground	lonely	simple

1. John had no wife or children, but he had his dog, Bobby. John and Bobby were always together. So, John was not alone, and he was not sad. He was not _____lonely_____.

2. Every day John took a long walk with his dog. Then he went home to his small house and cooked dinner. After dinner he sat in front of the fire. John had a _____ life.

3. John was buried in a cemetery in Edinburgh. After he was buried, Bobby stood at John's _____ and cried.

4. When the weather was cold or rainy, Bobby slept in a small house at the cemetery. But when the weather was warm, he slept outside, on the _____.

3. COMPREHENSION

◆ REMEMBERING DETAILS

One word in each sentence is not correct. Find the word and cross it out. Write the correct word.

1. Two friends lived together in a ~~big~~ *small* house in Scotland.

2. Their names were John and Sammy.

3. In the spring of 1958, John got sick and died.

4. He was buried in a cemetery in Edinburgh, Ireland.

5. Bobby lived in the cemetery for four years.

6. When Bobby died, friends buried him in a large grave.

7. Bobby, John's best friend, was a man.

◆ REVIEWING THE STORY

Complete each sentence. Then read the story again and check your answers.

John and Bobby lived together in a small house. They were not

_____*rich*_____, but they were happy. They had a warm
    1.

_____ when it was cold outside. They had good food
    2.

to eat when they were _____. They were never
    3.

_____ because they had each other.
    4.

After John died, Bobby lived in the cemetery. When the weather was cold or

_____, he slept in a small house at the cemetery. When the
    5.

_____ was warm, he slept on the ground near John's grave.
    6.

He lived in the cemetery for 14 _____, until he died in 1872.
    7.

◆ FINDING CLUES IN THE STORY

When did you know that Bobby was a dog—at the end of the story, or before the end? Which sentences in the story tell you that *maybe* Bobby was a dog? Underline them. Then read the sentences to the class.

4. WRITING/DISCUSSION

Bobby was a famous dog. People came to the cemetery to see him and bring him food. After he died, the people of Edinburgh put a statue of Bobby outside the cemetery.

Bobby died more than 100 years ago, but he is still famous. Every year thousands of tourists go to Edinburgh to see Bobby's grave and his statue.

The Statue of Bobby

A. Think about a city you know very well. Is there a place tourists always visit—a building, a park, a bridge, or a statue? Draw a picture of it. Then write about it. Complete the sentences.

The name of this place is _____.

It is in _____.

Many people go there because _____

_____.

I think it is _____.

B. Read your sentences to a partner. Show your partner your drawing. Tell your partner a little more about the place you drew.

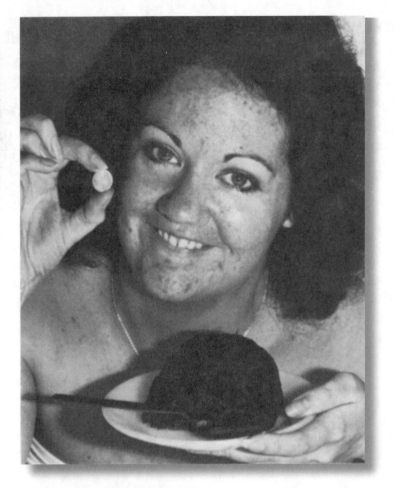

1. PRE-READING

Look at the picture.

▸ What is the woman holding in her right hand?

▸ What is she holding in her left hand?

Read the title of the story. Look at the picture again.

▸ What do you think this story is about?

▸ Can you guess what happens?

The Coin

It was December 25. Marie Orr, a 13-year-old Australian girl, was happy. It was Christmas, and Marie's mother was making a special cake for dessert. Her mother put four small coins into the cake; then she baked it. The four coins were for good luck.

After dinner Marie and her family ate the cake. They found three coins in the cake and put them on the table. Where was the fourth coin? It was missing, but Marie's mother didn't notice.

After Christmas Marie got sick. She coughed, and she couldn't speak. After six weeks, she felt better, but she still couldn't speak. Marie's parents took her to the hospital.

Doctors at the hospital looked at Marie. They took an x-ray of her throat. Marie's parents asked the doctors, "Why can't Marie speak?" The doctors said, "We don't know. Maybe she will speak again. Maybe she won't. We're sorry, but we can't help her."

For 12 years, Marie didn't speak. She grew up, she got a job, and she got married. But she never spoke.

One day, when Marie was 25 years old, she got a sore throat at work. She began to cough. She coughed up something small and black. What was it? Marie didn't know. She took it to the hospital. A doctor at the hospital said, "This is a coin!"

The doctor told Marie, "I think you can speak again." Marie went to a special doctor, and soon she was talking.

What a story Marie can tell!

2. VOCABULARY

Complete the sentences with the words below.

coins	coughed	missing	notice	throat

1. At Christmas many Australians put money in their cakes. Marie's mother put four small _____*coins*_____ in her cake.

2. There were only three coins on the table. Where was the fourth coin? It wasn't there. It was _____.

3. Marie's mother saw three coins on the table. One coin was missing, but she didn't pay attention. She didn't _____ that the coin was missing.

4. Marie got sick. She _____, and she couldn't speak.

5. Why couldn't Marie speak? The doctors didn't know, so they took an x-ray of her _____.

3. COMPREHENSION

◆ UNDERSTANDING THE MAIN IDEA

Circle the letter of the best answer.

1. Marie didn't speak because
   a. a coin was in her throat.
   b. she didn't want to.
   c. a doctor said, "We can't help her."

2. Now Marie can
   a. work again.
   b. bake cakes.
   c. speak again.

◆ REMEMBERING DETAILS

One word in each sentence is not correct. Find the word and cross it out. Write the correct word.

1. Marie Orr, a 13-year-old ~~French~~ *Australian* girl, was happy.

2. Her mother was making a special pie for dessert.

3. Marie's mother put four small spoons into the cake for good luck.

4. After breakfast Marie and her family ate the cake.

5. They found three coins in the cake and put them on the floor.

6. The sixth coin was missing, but Marie's mother didn't notice.

7. For 12 days, Marie didn't speak.

8. When she was 25 years old, Marie coughed up the cake, and she could speak again.

◆ UNDERSTANDING A SUMMARY

Imagine this: You want to tell the story "The Coin" to a friend. You want to tell the story quickly, in only four sentences. Which four sentences tell the story best? Check (✓) your answer.

☐ 1. Many Australians put coins in their Christmas cakes for good luck. Marie's mother put four small coins in her cake; then she baked it. After dinner Marie and her family ate the cake. They found three coins in the cake and put them on the table.

☐ 2. When she was 13 years old, Marie ate a piece of cake with a coin in it. The coin stayed in Marie's throat, but she didn't know it. She didn't speak for 12 years. When she was 25 years old, she coughed up the coin, and she could speak again.

4. DISCUSSION

In Australia many people put coins in their Christmas cakes; it is a good-luck custom.

Think about these questions. Talk about good-luck customs with your classmates.

▸ What are some good-luck customs in your family or from your native country?

▸ Do good-luck customs really bring good luck?

▸ Do you have a story about a good-luck custom?

5. WRITING

A. Answer the questions.

1. Marie liked Christmas very much. It was her favorite holiday. What is your favorite holiday?

   _____

2. Christmas is in December. When is your favorite holiday?

   _____

3. Red and green are the colors for Christmas in the United States. Does your favorite holiday have special colors? What are they?

   _____

4. Marie's mother made a cake for dessert. Do you eat anything special on your favorite holiday? What do you eat?

   _____

   _____

5. Marie's mother put coins in the cake. That was special; she did that only at Christmas. What special things do you do on your favorite holiday?

   _____

   _____

   _____

   _____

B. Take turns reading the sentences you wrote to a partner. Tell your partner a little more about your favorite holiday.

UNIT 10

1. PRE-READING

Look at the pictures.

▶ What sport does the man like?

▶ Can you guess how he feels?

Read the title of the story. Look at the pictures again.

▶ What do you think this story is about?

▶ Can you guess what happens?

Love or Baseball?

Joe Vitelli was excited. He liked to watch baseball, and his favorite team was going to play Saturday night. It was a championship game—the biggest game of the year. He was thinking about the game. "Maybe I'll invite some friends to my apartment," he thought. "We can eat pizza and watch the game on TV." Then the phone rang. It was Joe's girlfriend.

"Hi!" she said. "I bought my dress today."

"Your dress?" Joe asked.

"Yes, the dress for the dance," she answered. "Remember? You're taking me to the dance Saturday night."

"Oh, no," Joe thought. "I forgot: The dance is Saturday night."

"Joe?" his girlfriend asked. "You're taking me to the dance, right?"

"Right!" Joe said. "See you Saturday night."

Joe hung up the phone. What bad luck! The baseball game and the dance were on the same night! Joe didn't want to go to the dance. He wanted to watch the baseball game. The next day, he called his girlfriend.

"I'm sorry," he told her. "I can't go dancing Saturday night. Today I was playing football, and I broke my leg."

"Oh, no! Poor Joe!" his girlfriend said.

On Saturday night, Joe's girlfriend went to the dance alone, and he watched the baseball game on TV. It was a great game, and his team won. But now Joe had a problem. He and his girlfriend went to the same small university, and he saw her almost every day. A broken leg is in a cast. Joe didn't really have a broken leg, so his leg wasn't in a cast.

Joe bought a big white bandage and put it on his leg. Then he rented a wheelchair. Every day a friend pushed him in the wheelchair from his apartment to the university. For two weeks, Joe's plan worked perfectly. Then he got caught.

He went shopping without his bandage and without his wheelchair. He was walking through the store when his girlfriend saw him.

Joe doesn't have a girlfriend anymore. Now he has a lot of time to watch baseball games, and he is free every Saturday night.

2. VOCABULARY

Complete the sentences with the words below.

almost	got caught	hung up	rent

1. After Joe talked to his girlfriend, he _____*hung up*_____ the phone.

2. Joe saw his girlfriend on Mondays, Wednesdays, Thursdays, Fridays, and Saturdays. He saw her _____ every day.

3. Joe didn't want to buy a wheelchair because he needed it for only six weeks. So, he paid $20 every week to _____ a wheelchair.

4. Joe's girlfriend saw him at the store and thought, "He doesn't really have a broken leg!" Joe _____.

3. COMPREHENSION

◆ **UNDERSTANDING WORD GROUPS**

Read each group of words. One word in each group doesn't belong. Find the word and cross it out.

hung up ~~baseball~~ phone called rang	championship team shopping play game	cast broken leg bandage pizza wheelchair	Saturday night the next day perfectly today every day

◆ **REVIEWING THE STORY**

Complete each sentence. Then read the story again and check your answers.

Joe was excited because his favorite baseball _____*team*_____
1.
was going to play Saturday night. His girlfriend wanted to go to

a _____ Saturday night. He called her and said, "I'm sorry.
2.
I can't take you dancing because I broke my _____."
3.

Now Joe had a problem. A broken leg is in a _____.
4.
He put a big white _____ on his leg, and he rented
5.
a _____.
6.

One day Joe went shopping _____ his bandage and
7.
wheelchair. His girlfriend saw him. Now Joe has a lot of time to watch
baseball games because he doesn't have a _____ anymore.
8.

◆ **UNDERSTANDING TIME RELATIONSHIPS**

Complete the sentences. Write the letter of your answer on the line.

1. The baseball game and the dance were __c__

2. Joe called his girlfriend and said, "I broke my leg ____

3. Joe and his girlfriend went to the same university, and he saw her ____

4. Joe's plan worked perfectly ____

5. Now Joe is free ____

a. for two weeks.

b. every Saturday night.

c. on Saturday night.

d. today."

e. almost every day.

4. WRITING / DISCUSSION

Joe liked to watch baseball. How about you? What do you like to do?

A. Complete only the first part of each sentence. For example:

I like to _____play soccer_____, and so does _____.

1. I like to _____, and so does _____.

2. I like to _____, and so does _____.

3. I like to _____, and so does _____.

4. I like to _____, and so does _____.

B. Walk around the room and find people who like to do what you like to do. (You will need to ask, "Do you like to . . . ?") Write their names on the lines. For example:

I like to _____play soccer_____, and so does _____José Luis_____.

1. PRE-READING

Look at the picture.

▸ What do you see?

▸ What is this place?

Read the title of the story. Look at the picture again.

▸ What do you think this story is about?

▸ Can you guess what happens?

Buried Alive

In 1865, in a small town in Germany, a little boy was very sick. His name was Max Hoffman.

"Will our son die?" Max's parents asked the doctor.

"Maybe," the doctor said quietly. "Stay with Max. Keep him warm. That's all you can do."

For three days, Max lay in his bed. Then he died. He was only five years old.

Max's parents buried their son in the town cemetery. That night Max's mother had a terrible dream. She dreamed that Max was moving in his coffin. She screamed in her sleep.

"Shh, shh," her husband said. "It's all right. You had a bad dream."

The next night, Max's mother screamed in her sleep again. She had the same terrible dream.

On the third night, Max's mother had another bad dream. She dreamed that Max was crying.

She got out of bed and got dressed. "Quick! Get dressed," she told her husband. "We're going to the cemetery. I want to see Max. I want to dig up his coffin."

At four o'clock in the morning, Max's parents and a neighbor hurried to the cemetery. They dug up Max's coffin and opened it. There was Max. He looked dead. But something was different. When Max's parents buried him, he was lying on his back. Now he was lying on his side.

Max's father carried Max home. Then he ran to get the doctor. For an hour, the doctor rubbed whiskey on Max's lips and warmed his body. Then Max opened his eyes. Max was alive! A week later, he was playing with his friends.

Max Hoffman died—really died—in the United States in 1953. He was 93 years old.

2. VOCABULARY

Complete the sentences with the words below.

buried	dug up	hurried	lay	terrible

1. Max was very sick. He couldn't walk. He _____*lay*_____ in his bed.

2. After Max died, his parents _____ him in the town cemetery.

3. Max's mother had a very bad dream: She dreamed that Max was moving in his coffin.

   It was a _____ dream.

4. When Max's parents and a neighbor went to the cemetery, they walked fast. They

   _____ to the cemetery.

5. Max's parents and a neighbor took Max's coffin out of the ground.

   They _____ the coffin.

3. COMPREHENSION

◆ REMEMBERING DETAILS

One word in each sentence is not correct. Find the word and cross it out. Write the correct word.

1. In 1865, in a small town in ~~France~~, a little boy was very sick. *(Germany)*

2. For three months, Max lay in his bed; then he died.

3. Max's parents buried their daughter in the town cemetery.

4. That night Max's mother had a wonderful dream.

5. She laughed in her sleep.

6. Max's parents and a neighbor dug up the coffin and closed it.

7. When Max's parents buried him, he was lying on his back; now he was lying on his stomach.

8. Max's father carried him home and ran to get the neighbor.

9. The doctor rubbed whiskey on Max's ears and warmed his body.

10. A year later, Max was playing with his friends.

◆ UNDERSTANDING TIME AND PLACE

Read the phrases from the story. Which phrases tell you *when* something happened? Write them in the *WHEN* column. Which phrases tell you *where* something happened? Write them in the *WHERE* column.

in 1953   in Germany

in a small town   in 1865

in the United States   at four o'clock in the morning

the next night   in his bed

in the town cemetery   a week later

WHEN	*WHERE*
in 1953	in a small town

◆ UNDERSTANDING QUOTATIONS

Who said it? Match the sentences and the people. Write the letter of your answer on the line.

_c_ **1.** "Will our son die?"   **a.** Max's mother

____ **2.** "Stay with Max and keep him warm."   **b.** Max's father

____ **3.** "Shh, shh. It's all right."   **c.** Max's parents

____ **4.** "I want to dig up Max's coffin."   **d.** the doctor

4. DISCUSSION

A. Max Hoffman was buried for more than two days. Then his parents dug up his coffin. Max was alive! Do you think that's possible? Is this story true? Raise your hands and vote. How many students think Max Hoffman's story is possible? How many think it's impossible?

B. Max's mother dreamed about Max. Think about your dreams. With the help of your teacher, read the sentences below and circle *YES* or *NO*.

a. In the morning, I remember my dreams.	YES	NO
b. I have the same dream again and again.	YES	NO
c. I dreamed something—and then it happened.	YES	NO
d. I know a superstition about dreams. (For example: If you dream about snakes, you will get money.)	YES	NO
e. I sometimes speak English in my dreams.	YES	NO

Read your *YES* answers to a partner. Tell your partner a little more about your dreams.

5. WRITING

When Max Hoffman was an old man, he told his story to many people. People often asked Max questions.

Imagine that you are Max Hoffman. Answer the following questions on your own paper.

1. What happened when you were five years old?   *I "died."*

2. Where did your parents bury you?

3. What did your mother dream?

4. Who went to the cemetery and dug up your coffin?

5. Who carried you home?

6. What did the doctor do?

7. What were you doing a week later?

1. PRE-READING

Look at the picture.

▸ Where does this woman work?

▸ What does she sell?

▸ How much money can people win in the California State Lottery?

Read the title of the story. Look at the picture again.

▸ What do you think this story is about?

▸ Can you guess what happens?

The Winning Ticket

Therese Costabile is a cashier at a big drugstore in Cupertino, California. People can buy medicine at the drugstore. They can buy makeup, shampoo, watches, candy, and many other things, too. They pay Ms. Costabile for the things they buy.

At the drugstore, people can also buy tickets for the California State Lottery. They pay one dollar for a lottery ticket. There are pictures on the ticket. Some pictures are winning pictures, and some pictures are losing pictures. Most people win nothing. Some people win $2. A few lucky people win thousands of dollars.

One day Ms. Costabile was working at the drugstore. She sold three lottery tickets to a woman. The woman looked at the pictures on the tickets. Then she threw the tickets on the counter and walked away. "These are losing tickets," she thought.

Ms. Costabile picked up the tickets and looked at them. She was surprised. Then she was excited. One ticket was a winning ticket!

"Excuse me!" Ms. Costabile called to the woman. "You won $50,000!"

The woman walked back to the counter. She took the winning ticket and looked at it. "You're right," she said. "I won $50,000." The woman walked away slowly, in shock. Then she turned around. "Thanks," she said to Ms. Costabile.

Why did Ms. Costabile give the woman the ticket? Why didn't she keep the ticket? Didn't she want the $50,000?

"Of course I wanted the money," Ms. Costabile said. "But it was her ticket. It wasn't my ticket."

Ms. Costabile telephoned her mother and told her about the ticket.

"Well, I'm sorry that you aren't rich," her mother said. "But I'm happy that you're honest."

2. VOCABULARY

Complete the sentences with the words below.

cashier	counter	drugstore	lottery ticket	won

1. People buy medicine at a _____ *drugstore* _____.

2. When you buy something at a store, you pay the _____.

3. The cashier stands behind a high table. The high table is a _____.

4. People buy a _____ because they want to win money.

5. The state of California will give the woman $50,000 because she _____ the money in the lottery.

3. COMPREHENSION

◆ UNDERSTANDING WORD GROUPS

Read each group of words. One word in each group doesn't belong. Find the word and cross it out.

pay	potatoes	win	happy
counter	medicine	lottery	excited
~~weather~~	makeup	ticket	sick
cashier	shampoo	diet	lucky

◆ REMEMBERING DETAILS

One word in each sentence is not correct. Find the word and cross it out. Write the correct word.

1. Therese Costabile is a ~~manager~~ *cashier* at a big drugstore.

2. She sold three movie tickets to a woman.

3. The woman threw the tickets on the floor and walked away.

4. Ms. Costabile picked up the woman's money and looked at them.

5. Ms. Costabile called to the woman, "You won $5!"

6. The woman took the winning ticket and walked away slowly, in anger.

7. Ms. Costabile told her uncle about the winning ticket.

8. Her mother said, "Well, I'm sorry that you aren't rich, but I'm happy that you're friendly."

◆ UNDERSTANDING CAUSE AND EFFECT

Find the best way to complete each sentence. Write the letter of your answer on the line.

1. People pay Therese Costabile __c__

2. The woman threw the tickets on the counter ____

3. Ms. Costabile didn't keep the winning ticket ____

4. Ms. Costabile's mother was happy ____

a. because it wasn't her ticket.

b. because her daughter is honest.

c. because she is a cashier.

d. because she thought they were losing tickets.

4. DISCUSSION

1. Drugstores in the United States sell medicine and many other things. What things can people buy at drugstores in the United States? Make a list with your classmates. Are drugstores in your native country like drugstores in the United States?

2. Imagine this: You buy a lottery ticket. You think it is a losing ticket, so you throw it on the counter. The cashier says, "Wait! You won $50,000!" You take the lottery ticket and look at it. The cashier is right. You won $50,000. What do you do next?

Check (✓) your answer. Then discuss your answer with your classmates.

You . . .

☐ **a.** say "thank you" and walk away.

☐ **b.** give the cashier half the money—$25,000.

☐ **c.** give the cashier $_____.

☐ **d.** _____

(Write your own idea.)

5. WRITING

Imagine this: You win $50,000 in the lottery. What will you do with the money? Will you buy a car, go on a vacation, buy presents for everyone you know? Make a list of things you will buy or do.

With my $50,000, I will . . .

_____

_____

_____

_____

Read your list to a partner. Tell your partner why you want to buy or do the things on your list.

1. PRE-READING

Look at the pictures.

▸ What animal is this?

▸ Can you see the man in the photo on the left? What do you
   think he's doing?

Read the title of the story. Look at the pictures again.

▸ What do you think this story is about?

▸ Can you guess what happens?

Thank You

One morning a fisherman was fishing in the Pacific Ocean, about 18 miles from San Francisco. He saw something strange. There was a whale in the water, and it wasn't moving. Was the whale dead? The fisherman didn't think so. He moved his boat to take a closer look.

The whale wasn't dead. It was caught in fishing lines, and it couldn't move. It was a special whale—a humpback whale. There are only 6,000 humpback whales in the world. The fisherman called for help.

A few hours later, five men from San Francisco arrived to help. From their boat, they looked at the whale. They saw fishing lines everywhere. The fishing lines were around the whale's body, around its tail, and in its mouth. "We have to go into the water," the men said. "We have to cut the fishing lines."

The men looked at one another. The whale was very big, and it was dangerous. "If the whale moves its tail, it will kill us," they said. "I'll go in the water," one man said. "I'll go in, too," a second man said. "Me, too," a third man said. "Me, too," a fourth man said. The four men put on diving suits and jumped into the water. Each man held a knife in his hand. A fifth man, the captain of the boat, stayed in the boat.

The men began cutting the fishing lines. The whale watched them. One man was near the whale's eye. He saw the whale blink. But the whale didn't move.

One hour later, the men cut the last fishing line. The whale swam away. It swam in big circles and jumped into the air. Then it swam back to the men. Why was it swimming back? What was it going to do? The men in the water were afraid to move.

The whale swam to the first man and stopped. It pushed him gently with its nose. Then it swam to the second man, and the third man, and the fourth man. It pushed each man gently with its nose. Was the whale thanking the men? They thought so. They touched the whale with their hands and rubbed against it with their shoulders. "You're welcome," they told the whale. "You're very welcome."

2. VOCABULARY

Which words or pictures have the same meaning as the words in *italics*? Circle the letter of your answer.

1. Fishing lines were around the whale's *tail*.

2. The man is wearing a *diving suit*.
   a.   b.

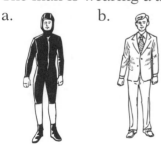

3. The whale *blinked*.
   a. closed its mouth and then opened it
   b. closed its eye and then opened it

4. Each man rubbed against the whale with his *shoulder*.

3. PRACTICING PRONUNCIATION

The underlined words are in the story. If you can say them correctly, you can say the words below them correctly, too. Practice with your teacher.

<u>hand</u>	<u>each</u>	<u>swam</u>	<u>stay</u>	<u>will</u>	<u>dead</u>
band	beach	slam	day	bill	bread
land	peach	spam	pay	fill	head
sand	reach	ham	play	kill	read (past tense)
stand	teach	jam	pray	pill	spread

4. COMPREHENSION

◆ **UNDERSTANDING THE MAIN IDEAS**

Circle the letter of the correct answer.

1. The fisherman moved his boat because
   a. he wanted to take a closer look at the whale.
   b. he was afraid of the whale.

2. The whale couldn't move because
   a. it was sick.
   b. it was caught in fishing lines.

3. Humpback whales are special because
   a. they are very big.
   b. there are only 6,000 in the world.

4. The men from San Francisco had to go into the water because
   a. they needed to take a closer look at the whale.
   b. they needed to cut the fishing lines.

5. The whale was dangerous because
   a. it could kill the men with its tail.
   b. it had very big teeth.

6. The whale swam back to the men because
   a. it wanted to thank them.
   b. it wanted food.

◆ **UNDERSTANDING A SUMMARY**

Imagine this: You want to tell the story "Thank You" to a friend. You want to tell the story quickly, in only five sentences. Which five sentences tell the story best? Check (✓) your answer.

☐ 1. A humpback whale was caught in fishing lines. Four men jumped into the water and cut the lines. The whale swam away but then swam back to the men. It pushed each man gently with its nose. It was saying "Thank you."

☐ 2. A fisherman was fishing in the Pacific Ocean about 18 miles from San Francisco. He saw a humpback whale in the water. The whale wasn't moving. It was caught in fishing lines. The fisherman called for help.

5. DISCUSSION/WRITING

A. In a small group, guess the answers to the questions about the humpback whale. Your group must decide on one answer to each question. Write short answers on the lines. Then look in the Answer Key. Were your group's guesses correct?

1. What color are humpback whales? ___black and white___

2. What do they eat? _____

3. How many kilograms of food does a humpback whale eat every day?

   _____

4. How many months is a female humpback whale pregnant?

   _____

5. How many kilograms does a baby humpback whale weigh when it is born? _____

6. What does a baby humpback whale eat during its first year of life?

   _____

B. On your own paper, write the correct answers to the questions above. Write your answers in complete sentences. For example:

1. *They are black and white.*

1. PRE-READING

Look at the picture.

▸ Where do you think this family is from?

▸ Can you guess how they feel?

Read the title of the story. Look at the picture again.

▸ What do you think this story is about?

▸ Can you guess what happens?

Together Again

Orestes Lorenzo was a pilot in the Cuban Air Force. Orestes liked the Air Force and he liked flying, but he didn't like living in Cuba. There was not enough freedom in Cuba. Orestes wanted to live in the United States, but the Cuban government told him, "No. You can't leave Cuba."

In March 1991, Orestes got into a Cuban Air Force jet and flew the jet to Florida. "I'm never going back to Cuba," he thought.

When Orestes flew to the United States, he left his wife and two sons in Cuba. Orestes thought, "My family can come to the United States later."

Orestes was wrong. The Cuban government told Orestes's wife, "You can't leave Cuba. Forget your husband."

For almost two years, Orestes lived in the United States, and his family lived in Cuba. Orestes was very unhappy. In Cuba he had his family, but he didn't have enough freedom. In the United States, he had freedom, but he didn't have his family.

One day Orestes got a letter from his son Alejandro. "Dear Daddy," Alejandro wrote.

"You are a pilot. Fly to Cuba! Take us to the United States in an airplane!"

Orestes read Alejandro's letter and began to think. "Maybe Alejandro has a good idea," he thought. "Maybe I *can* fly to Cuba and get my family."

Orestes wrote a letter to his wife, Victoria. In the letter, Orestes told Victoria, "On December 19 at 5:30, take the boys to our favorite beach for a picnic. Wear orange T-shirts. And watch the sky."

At 5:30 on December 19, Victoria and the two boys were at the beach. The boys were playing, but Victoria was watching the sky. She saw a small plane. It was flying low over a highway nearby. "Run to the highway!" she told the boys. "It's Daddy!"

Orestes was flying a small plane right over the highway. He flew over a car, a bus, and a truck. Then he landed on the highway. Victoria and the boys got into the plane, and the plane took off. Fifty minutes later, the Lorenzo family was in Florida.

Later Victoria said, "I knew he would come. I always knew it. I believe in him. I believe in love."

2. VOCABULARY

Which words or pictures have the same meaning as the words in *italics*? Circle the letter of your answer.

1. Orestes flew a *jet* to Florida.
   a. a fast airplane
   b. a small airplane

2. Orestes flew low over the *highway*.
   a. a big road between two cities
   b. a small street in a city

3. Orestes *landed* on the highway.

   a.   b.

4. Victoria and the boys got into the plane, and the plane *took off*.

   a.   b.

3. COMPREHENSION

◆ FINDING INFORMATION

What information is in the story? What information is not in the story?

There are two correct ways to complete each sentence. Circle the letters of the *two* correct answers.

1. In Cuba, Orestes liked
   (a.) flying.
   b. his house.
   (c.) the Air Force.

2. When Orestes flew to Florida, he thought,
   a. "The U.S. Air Force wants this jet."
   b. "I'm never going back to Cuba."
   c. "My family can come to the United States later."

3. The Cuban government told Orestes's wife,
   a. "You can't leave Cuba."
   b. "Forget your husband."
   c. "Your husband is dead."

4. After he read Alejandro's letter, Orestes thought,
   a. "Maybe Alejandro has a good idea."
   b. "I miss my son very much."
   c. "Maybe I *can* fly to Cuba and get my family."

5. In his letter to Victoria, Orestes wrote,
   a. "I bought a small plane."
   b. "Take the boys to our favorite beach for a picnic."
   c. "Wear orange T-shirts."

◆ MAKING CONNECTIONS

Find the best way to complete each sentence. Write the letter of your answer on the line.

1. Orestes thought, "My family can come to the United States later," but _b_

2. In Cuba Orestes had his family, but _____

3. In the United States, Orestes had freedom, but _____

4. On December 19, the boys were playing on the beach, but _____

a. he didn't have freedom.

b. the Cuban government told Orestes's wife, "You can't leave Cuba."

c. Victoria was watching the sky.

d. he didn't have his family.

◆ **REMEMBERING DETAILS**

One word in each sentence is not correct. Find the word and cross it out.
Write the correct word.

1. Orestes Lorenzo was a ~~mechanic~~ *pilot* in the Cuban Air Force.

2. Orestes didn't like living in Cuba because there was not enough peace.

3. Orestes got into a Cuban Air Force jet and flew the jet to California.

4. When Orestes flew to Florida, he left his wife and two daughters in Cuba.

5. For almost ten years, Orestes lived in the United States, and his family
   lived in Cuba.

4. WRITING / DISCUSSION

Orestes Lorenzo liked living in the United States because he had freedom.
He didn't like living in the United States because he didn't have his family.

**A. Are you living in the United States? What do you like about it? What
don't you like? Make two lists.**

IN THE UNITED STATES

I like . . .   I don't like . . .

_____   _____

_____   _____

**What about your native country? What do you like about it? What don't you
like? Make two lists.**

IN MY NATIVE COUNTRY

I like . . .   I don't like . . .

_____   _____

_____   _____

**B. Take turns reading your lists to a partner. Are your lists and your partner's
lists the same?**

1. PRE-READING

Look at the picture.

- ▸ Where is this?
- ▸ What is the man doing?
- ▸ How is the weather?

Read the title of the story. Look at the picture again.

- ▸ What do you think this story is about?
- ▸ Can you guess what happens?

Saved by the Bell

Nevado del Ruiz is a mountain in Colombia. It is 5,425 meters high, and it is popular with climbers. It is beautiful, but it is dangerous, too. The weather can change quickly on the mountain. One minute it is sunny, and the next minute it is cloudy. One minute it is warm, and the next minute it is cold.

On a sunny morning in June, Leonardo Diaz began climbing Nevado del Ruiz with some friends. On the second day of their climb, there was a snowstorm. It was difficult to walk in the snow, and it was difficult to see. The climbers decided to turn around and walk down the mountain. Leonardo stopped for a minute to get something out of his backpack. When he looked up, his friends were gone. He couldn't see them or their footprints in the snow. "Wait!" Leonardo shouted. But his friends couldn't hear him in the storm.

All day Leonardo continued down the mountain alone. That night he put up his tent, crawled inside, and slept. When he woke up the next morning, he was in big trouble. His clothes were not warm enough, so he was very cold. He was hungry, too, because he had no food left. He decided to call for help. He opened his backpack and took out his cell phone. It didn't work. Leonardo had no more prepaid minutes on his phone.

All morning Leonardo stayed in his tent and listened to the storm. He began to think, "Maybe I'll die on this mountain."

Then his cell phone rang.

"Hello?" he answered.

"Good afternoon," a woman said. "I'm calling from Bell South Phone Company. You have no minutes left on your cell phone. Would you like to buy more minutes?"

"Yes!" Leonardo shouted into the phone. "Please help me! I'm lost in a snowstorm on Nevado del Ruiz."

"Excuse me," the woman said. "I don't understand. Do you want to buy more minutes?"

"Yes, but not now!" Leonardo said. "I need help. I'm lost on a mountain."

"Stay where you are," the woman said. "I'll send for help."

Late that night, a rescue team arrived and helped Leonardo down the mountain.

Leonardo says he will probably try again to climb Nevado del Ruiz. But the next time, he will bring plenty of warm clothes and plenty of food. He will also bring a cell phone with plenty of prepaid minutes.

2. VOCABULARY

Complete the sentences with the words below.

crawled	plenty	shouted	trouble

1. Leonardo's tent was small, so Leonardo went inside on his hands and knees. He _____crawled_____ into his tent.

2. Leonardo was lost in a snowstorm. He was cold and hungry, too. He was in big _____.

3. Leonardo spoke loudly when he talked on the phone. "Help me!" he _____.

4. The next time Leonardo climbs the mountain, he will bring two jackets, a hat, and gloves. He will bring _____ of warm clothes.

59

3. COMPREHENSION

◆ REMEMBERING DETAILS

Read the summary of the story "Saved by the Bell." There are ten mistakes in the summary. Find the mistakes and cross them out. Write the correct words. (The first one is done for you.)

On a ~~cloudy~~ *sunny* morning in July, Leonardo and his family began climbing Nevado del Ruiz, a mountain in Peru. On the second day of their climb, they decided to turn around because there was a rainstorm. Leonardo stopped to get something out of his pocket. When he looked up, his friends were gone.

Leonardo was lost on the mountain. He tried to call for help on his radio, but it didn't work. He didn't have any more prepaid hours. He stayed in his tent and waited for the storm to stop. Then his cell phone rang. A man from the phone company asked Leonardo, "Do you want to buy more minutes for your cell phone?" Leonardo asked her for help, and she sent a ski team. They helped Leonardo down the mountain.

◆ UNDERSTANDING DIALOG

Below is the conversation between Leonardo and the woman from the phone company. Some words are missing from their conversation. Write the missing words on the lines. Then practice the conversation with a partner. One student is speaker A, and the other student is speaker B.

A: Hello?

B: Good afternoon. I'm calling from Bell South Phone Company. Would you like to buy more minutes for your _____*cell*_____ phone?

A: Yes! Please help me! I'm _____ in a snowstorm on Nevado del Ruiz.

B: Excuse me. I don't understand. Do you want to buy more _____?

A: Yes, but not now! I need _____. I'm lost on a mountain.

B: _____ where you are. I'll send for help.

Read each sentence on the left. Which sentence on the right gives you more information? Write the letter of your answer on the line.

_c_ **1.** Nevado del Ruiz is a mountain in Colombia.

a. One minute it is warm, and the next minute it is cold.

____ **2.** The weather can change quickly on the mountain.

b. He couldn't see them or their footprints.

____ **3.** There was a snowstorm.

c. It is 5,425 meters high.

____ **4.** Leonardo's friends were gone.

d. It had no more prepaid minutes.

____ **5.** Leonardo's cell phone didn't work.

e. It was difficult to walk, and it was difficult to see.

4. DISCUSSION

Leonardo was not prepared for an emergency on the mountain. He didn't have warm clothes, he didn't have enough food, and he didn't have any prepaid minutes left on his cell phone. Are *you* prepared for an emergency?

With your classmates, make a list of things you need in your home for an emergency (a flashlight, for example). Which things do you have? Tell the class.

5. WRITING

The weather on Nevado del Ruiz can be warm or cold, sunny or cloudy. How is the weather in your native city?

Write a few sentences about each season. For example:

In the fall, it is very beautiful. The temperature is usually 20 degrees Celsius, and the sky is clear. When the trees change to beautiful colors, we go to the mountains for picnics.

In the winter, _____

_____

In the spring, _____

_____

In the summer, _____

_____

In the fall, _____

_____

UNIT 16

1. PRE-READING

Look at the pictures.

▶ How old is this boy?

▶ Can you guess how he feels?

▶ How old is the man?

▶ Can you guess how he feels?

Read the title of the story. Look at the pictures again.

▶ What do you think this story is about?

▶ Can you guess what happens?

This Is the Place for Me

Walter Polovchak, a 12-year-old boy, was listening to rock 'n' roll music. "Turn off that garbage!" his father shouted. Walter turned off the music.

Walter and his family lived in Chicago, Illinois, but they were from Ukraine. Walter's father wasn't happy in Chicago. He didn't like American rock 'n' roll. He didn't like his job. He didn't like the weather. He didn't like the food or water. "Coming to the United States was a big mistake," Walter's father said. "We're going back home."

Walter didn't want to leave Chicago. He liked his school, and he liked American sports. He liked American food, too. Walter was happy in the United States. His 18-year-old sister Natalie was happy, too. Walter and Natalie packed their clothes and went to live with a cousin. "We're not going back to Ukraine," they said.

Walter's parents said, "Natalie is 18. She can stay in the United States. But Walter is only 12. He has to come with us." Walter's parents called the police. "We want our son," they told the police. The police didn't know what to do. They called the U.S. Immigration and Naturalization Service (INS). The INS made a decision. They said, "Walter can stay in the United States."

Walter's parents went back to Ukraine without Walter and Natalie. But first they hired a lawyer. "We want our son," they told the lawyer. "Go to court. Help us get our son back."

The U.S. courts said, "Walter's parents are right. The INS is wrong. Walter has to go back to Ukraine." But Walter didn't go back. When the court finally made its decision, Walter Polovchak was 18 years old. He was an adult, so he could live where he wanted to live. He stayed in the United States.

Walter Polovchak is in his early 40s now. He is married and has a son. He still lives in Chicago, and his parents are still in Ukraine. Walter and his family visit his parents sometimes. He says he is sorry they live far away, but he is not sorry he stayed in the United States. "I couldn't go back to Ukraine," he says. "In my heart, I always knew that this was the place for me."

2. VOCABULARY

Which sentence has the same meaning as the sentence in the story? Circle the letter of your answer.

1. Walter was listening to rock 'n' roll music. His father didn't like rock 'n' roll. *"Turn off that garbage!" he shouted.*
   a. "Turn off that beautiful music!" he said quietly.
   b. "Turn off that terrible music!" he said loudly.

2. Walter and Natalie *packed their clothes* and went to live with a cousin.
   a. Walter and Natalie put their clothes in a suitcase.
   b. Walter and Natalie gave their clothes to their parents.

3. Walter's parents went back to Ukraine *without* Walter and Natalie.
   a. Walter's parents went back to Ukraine. Walter and Natalie went back to Ukraine, too.
   b. Walter's parents went back to Ukraine. Walter and Natalie stayed in the United States.

4. Walter's parents *hired* a lawyer.
   a. Walter's parents told the lawyer, "Work for us. We will pay you."
   b. Walter's parents told the lawyer, "We don't need your help. Please go away."

3. COMPREHENSION

◆ FINDING INFORMATION

What information is in the story? What information is not in the story?

There are two correct ways to complete each sentence. Circle the letters of the *two* correct answers.

1. The Polovchak family
   a. was from Ukraine.
   b. had a lot of money.
   c. lived in Chicago.

2. Walter's father
   a. wasn't happy in Chicago.
   b. wanted to go back home.
   c. was 45 years old.

3. Walter
   a. was a good student.
   b. was 12 years old.
   c. didn't want to leave Chicago.

4. Walter's parents wanted their son back, so they
   a. gave him many gifts.
   b. called the police.
   c. hired a lawyer.

5. Today Walter Polovchak
   a. has a good job.
   b. is in his early 40s.
   c. still lives in Chicago.

◆ UNDERSTANDING CAUSE AND EFFECT

Find the best way to complete each sentence. Write the letter of your answer on the line.

1. Walter's father wasn't happy in Chicago, so ___b___

2. Walter and Natalie didn't want to go back to Ukraine, so ___

3. Walter's parents said, "Natalie is 18, so ___

4. When the court finally made its decision, Walter was 18, so ___

a. she can stay in the United States."

b. he said, "We're going back to Ukraine."

c. he could live where he wanted to live.

d. they packed their clothes and went to live with a cousin.

◆ LOOKING FOR DETAILS

What didn't Walter's father like? Find the words in the story.

American rock 'n' roll

What did Walter like? Find the words in the story.

his school

4. DISCUSSION

1. The INS said, "Walter can stay in the United States." But the U.S. courts said, "Walter has to go back to Ukraine."

   Raise your hands and vote. How many students think the INS was right? How many think the courts were right?

2. After six months in the United States, Walter's father wanted to go back to Ukraine. He was not happy in Chicago.

   That is not unusual. Many people are unhappy after six months in a new country.

   When people arrive in a new country, they are usually happy. A few weeks or a few months later, many people are sad. (Why do you think they are sad?) After one or two years in the new country, they are usually OK.

   Are you in a new country now? How do you feel? Happy? Sad? OK? Going down? Coming up? Where are you now? Put an X on the line.

   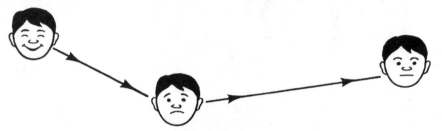

   Show a partner where you put your X. Why did you put your X there? Tell your partner.

5. WRITING

Are you in a new country now? Answer the questions. Complete the sentences. OR Imagine this: You are Walter's father. You are living in the United States. Answer the questions.

1. How did you feel when you arrived? (excited? sad? afraid? nervous?)

   When I came here, I felt ＿＿＿＿＿＿ because ＿＿＿＿＿＿＿＿＿

   ＿＿＿＿＿＿＿＿＿＿＿＿＿＿＿＿＿＿＿＿＿＿＿＿＿＿＿＿.

2. How do you feel now?

   Now I feel ＿＿＿＿＿＿ because ＿＿＿＿＿＿＿＿＿＿＿＿

   ＿＿＿＿＿＿＿＿＿＿＿＿＿＿＿＿＿＿＿＿＿＿＿＿＿＿＿＿.

3. How will you feel in one year?

   Maybe I will feel ＿＿＿＿＿＿ because ＿＿＿＿＿＿＿＿＿＿

   ＿＿＿＿＿＿＿＿＿＿＿＿＿＿＿＿＿＿＿＿＿＿＿＿＿＿＿＿.

1. PRE-READING

Look at the pictures.

▸ How old is the woman?

▸ Where does she live?

▸ Can you guess how she feels?

▸ What kind of ring is she wearing on her hand?

Read the title of the story. Look at the pictures again.

▸ What do you think this story is about?

▸ Can you guess what happens?

Nicole's Party

On the morning of her wedding day, Nicole Contos got a phone call from her fiancé. His name was Tasos. "I love you, Nicole," Tasos said. "But I'm really nervous. My legs are like jelly."

"I'm a little nervous, too," Nicole said. "Don't worry. Everything will be fine. I love you, too."

That afternoon Nicole put on her white wedding dress and went to a church in New York City. At the church, she held a bouquet of flowers in her hands and waited.

At the front of the church, a minister stood and waited.

In the church, 250 guests sat quietly. They were the friends and family of Nicole and Tasos. They waited, too.

Everyone was waiting for Tasos. They waited, and waited, and waited.

Finally, Tasos's best friend walked into the church. "Tasos isn't coming," he whispered to Nicole's brother. "He doesn't want to get married. He changed his mind."

Nicole's brother told Nicole that Tasos wasn't coming. First, Nicole cried. Then she thought about the wedding guests. At a hotel near the church, ten cooks were making dinner for them, and a band was getting ready to play music.

"Tell the guests there isn't going to be a wedding today," Nicole told her brother. "But tell them there *is* going to be a party. Tell them to go to the hotel."

Nicole went home and put on a black party dress. Then she went to the hotel. As the guests ate dinner and wedding cake, Nicole walked from table to table and smiled. "Thank you for coming," she told her guests. After dinner, the band played music. Nicole was the first one on the dance floor. She danced with her brother. Inside, her heart was breaking. But all evening, she never stopped smiling.

Later Nicole said, "I'll be OK. Something good came from this experience: I learned how strong I really am."

At the end of the evening, Nicole's brother raised his glass and said, "Let's all drink to Nicole. She's a great woman. Someday a lucky man will marry her, and she will make him really, really happy."

2. VOCABULARY

Complete the sentences with the words below.

changed his mind	fiancé	guests	wedding

1. Nicole was going to marry Tasos. He was her _____*fiancé*_____.

2. They were going to get married in New York City. The _____ was at a church.

3. Many people came to see the wedding. They were the wedding _____.

4. First Tasos said, "I want to marry Nicole." Then he said, "I don't want to marry Nicole." He _____.

3. PRACTICING PRONUNCIATION

The underlined words are in the story. If you can say them correctly, you can say the words below them correctly, too. Practice with your teacher.

day	went	then	tell	cook	make
May	bent	men	cell	book	bake
pay	dent	pen	fell	hook	cake
say	rent	ten	sell	look	lake
way	sent	when	well	took	take

4. COMPREHENSION

◆ UNDERSTANDING THE MAIN IDEAS

Circle the letter of the best answer.

1. On the morning of their wedding day, Tasos called Nicole and said,
   a. "I'm going to be really late."
   b. "I'm really nervous."
   c. "I'm really happy."

2. Tasos didn't come to the church because
   a. he was sick.
   b. he had a car accident.
   c. he didn't want to get married.

3. When Tasos didn't come to the church, Nicole
   a. looked for him all over New York City.
   b. went home and stayed in bed.
   c. cried but then went to the hotel for a party.

4. From her experience, Nicole learned that
   a. she was really strong.
   b. weddings are expensive.
   c. all men are nervous about getting married.

◆ UNDERSTANDING QUOTATIONS

Who said it? Match the sentences and the people. Write the letter of your answer on the line.

__b__ 1. "Let's all drink to Nicole."   **a.** Nicole

_____ 2. "Tasos doesn't want to get married."   **b.** Nicole's brother

_____ 3. "My legs are like jelly."   **c.** Tasos's best friend

_____ 4. "Something good came from this experience."   **d.** Tasos

5. DISCUSSION

**Look at the pictures below. You often see these things at weddings in the
United States. Do you see these things at weddings in your native country?
Which things are the same? Which are different? Tell the class.**

6. WRITING

Write four sentences about weddings in your native country. For example:

Sometimes a wedding lasts for two or three days.
Sometimes many people get married at the same time.

1. _____

2. _____

3. _____

4. _____

UNIT 18

1. PRE-READING

Look at the picture.

▶ Is the water warm or cold?

▶ Who is in the water?

Read the title of the story. Look at the picture again.

▶ What do you think this story is about?

▶ Can you guess what happens?

A Strong Little Boy

Chicago, Illinois, is next to a big, beautiful lake—Lake Michigan. In the summer, Lake Michigan is warm and blue. People lie on the beaches and swim in the water. In the winter, Lake Michigan is cold and gray. Snow covers the beaches, and ice covers the water.

On a cold January day, a little boy and his father were playing in the snow on a Chicago beach. The boy was Jimmy Tontlewicz. He was four years old.

Jimmy was playing with a sled. He pushed the sled down a small hill. The sled went onto the ice of Lake Michigan. Jimmy ran after the sled. He ran onto the ice. Suddenly the ice broke, and Jimmy fell into the cold water.

Jimmy's father jumped into the water. He couldn't find Jimmy. Minutes went by. He still couldn't find Jimmy. "My kid is dead! My kid is dead!" he screamed.

Men from the Chicago Fire Department arrived. Twenty minutes later, they found Jimmy and pulled him out of the water. Jimmy was not breathing, and his heart was not beating. He was dead.

At the beach, paramedics worked on Jimmy for one hour. He began to breathe, and his heart began to beat again. The paramedics rushed Jimmy to the hospital.

Doctors at the hospital put Jimmy in bed. They put him on a cold mattress because they wanted his body to warm up slowly. They gave him some medicine because they wanted him to sleep.

After eight days in the hospital, Jimmy woke up, but he couldn't walk or talk. He stayed in the hospital for six weeks. Every day he got better. Then he went to another hospital. He stayed there for seven weeks. He began to walk, talk, and play again.

Jimmy was in the water for over 20 minutes. He couldn't breathe in the water. He couldn't get any oxygen. But today he is alive and healthy. How is it possible?

Jimmy is alive because the water was ice cold. Usually the brain needs a lot of oxygen. But when it's very cold, the brain slows down. It does not need much oxygen. So the ice cold water saved Jimmy.

Jimmy's father has another reason. He says, "Jimmy is alive today because he is a fighter. He is a strong little boy."

2. VOCABULARY

Which sentence has the same meaning as the sentence in the story? Circle the letter of your answer.

1. Snow *covers* the beaches, and ice *covers* the water.
   a. Snow is on the beaches, and ice is on the water.
   b. Snow is near the beaches, and ice is near the water.

2. The paramedics *worked on* Jimmy for one hour.
   a. The doctor's assistants helped Jimmy work again. Jimmy worked for one hour.
   b. The doctor's assistants helped Jimmy breathe again. They helped Jimmy for one hour.

3. The paramedics *rushed* Jimmy to the hospital.
   a. The paramedics took Jimmy to the hospital. They drove fast.
   b. The paramedics took Jimmy to the hospital. They drove slowly.

4. Jimmy was in the water for *over 20 minutes*.
   a. Jimmy was in the water for more than 20 minutes.
   b. Jimmy was in the water for 20 minutes.

71

3. COMPREHENSION

◆ **FINDING INFORMATION**

Read the questions. Find the answers in the story. Write the answers.

1. Was it a cold day in January or a warm day in May?

   It was a cold day in January.

2. Were Jimmy and his father playing in a Chicago park or on a Chicago beach?

   _____

3. Did Jimmy run onto the ice or into the water?

   _____

4. Did the sled break, or did the ice break?

   _____

5. Who pulled Jimmy out of the water, his father or firefighters?

   _____

6. Was Jimmy in the water for over two minutes or for over twenty minutes?

   _____

◆ **UNDERSTANDING CAUSE AND EFFECT**

Find the best way to complete each sentence. Write the letter of your answer on the line.

1. Jimmy fell into the cold water *d*

2. Paramedics worked on Jimmy _____

3. Doctors put Jimmy on a cold mattress _____

4. Doctors at the hospital gave Jimmy some medicine _____

5. Jimmy is alive today _____

a. because they wanted Jimmy to warm up slowly.

b. because they wanted Jimmy to sleep.

c. because the water was ice cold.

d. because the ice broke.

e. because they wanted Jimmy to breathe again.

◆ **UNDERSTANDING WORD GROUPS**

Read each group of words. One word in each group doesn't belong.
Find the word and cross it out.

ice	paramedics	alive	mattress
cold	hospital	got better	garden
~~hot~~	pilot	strong	wake up
winter	medicine	healthy	sleep
snow	doctors	nervous	bed

4. DISCUSSION

Do you have any experience with fire departments, rescues, ambulances,
paramedics, or hospitals?

**With the help of your teacher or your dictionary, read the sentences below
and circle YES or NO.**

1. I called the fire department.	YES	NO
2. I called an ambulance.	YES	NO
3. I saw a rescue.	YES	NO
4. Someone rescued me.	YES	NO
5. I saw paramedics. They were working on someone.	YES	NO
6. Paramedics worked on me.	YES	NO
7. I went to the hospital in an ambulance.	YES	NO
8. Someone in my family went to the hospital in an ambulance.	YES	NO
9. I was a patient in a hospital.	YES	NO
10. Someone in my family was a patient in a hospital.	YES	NO
11. I know a true story about a rescue.	YES	NO

**Read your YES sentences to a partner. Tell your partner about your
experiences.**

5. WRITING

When Jimmy was in the hospital, he got cards and letters from people all over
the world. "Get well soon," people wrote. "We are thinking of you."

**Imagine this: Your friend is in the hospital. Maybe your friend is sick, or
maybe your friend had an accident. What can you write to your friend?
Make a list of possible sentences with your classmates. Your teacher will
write your sentences on the board.**

**Now, on your own paper, write a short letter (two or three sentences) to
your friend in the hospital.**

UNIT 19

1. PRE-READING

Look at the picture on the right.

▸ What kind of medal is that?

▸ Can you read the date on the medal?

▸ Can you read the city on the medal?

Read the title of the story. Look at the picture again.

▸ What do you think this story is about?

▸ Can you guess what happens?

The Champion

In 1938, before his accident, Károly Takács had big plans. He wanted to be an Olympic champion. He was very good at shooting a pistol, and he was on the Hungarian pistol-shooting team. "Maybe I can win a gold medal at the next Olympics," he thought. Then the accident happened.

Károly was a soldier in the Hungarian army. One day he was practicing with grenades. He picked up a grenade and held it in his hand. Before he could throw it, the grenade exploded. Doctors had to cut off Károly's right hand—his shooting hand.

Károly was in the hospital for a month. Then he went home to rest. He was very depressed. He didn't want to see his friends, and he never went out. He stayed in bed almost all day. His wife was worried about him.

One day Károly came out of the bedroom with a pistol in his left hand. "What are you going to do with the pistol?" his wife asked. Károly didn't answer. He walked toward the door. "Károly, where are you going?" his wife asked. He didn't say anything. He went out the door and walked quickly into the woods behind their house. Károly's wife heard a gunshot in the woods, and she almost fainted. Then she heard another shot, and another, and another. Károly was practicing in the woods. He was learning to shoot with his left hand.

A year later, Károly went to the Hungarian National Pistol-Shooting Competition. When people saw him, they were surprised. "We're sorry about your accident," they told him. "Did you come to watch the competition?"

"No," Károly said. "I came here to shoot." He won the competition. After that, he began to think about the Olympics again.

In 1940 and 1944, there were no Olympic Games because of World War II. So Károly had eight years to practice. In 1948, he went to the Olympics with the Hungarian team. He won the gold medal in pistol shooting. In 1952, he returned to the Olympics and won another gold medal in pistol shooting.

Before his accident, Károly Takács had big plans: He wanted to be an Olympic champion. After his accident, he became an Olympic champion, and more: In Hungary, he was a national hero.

2. VOCABULARY

Complete the sentences with the words below.

army	happened	medal
exploded	hero	pistol

1. Károly Takács was good at shooting a _____*pistol*_____.

2. He was a soldier in the _____.

3. The grenade _____.

4. The accident _____ in 1938.

5. He won an Olympic gold _____.

6. When he returned to Hungary, he was a national _____.

3. COMPREHENSION

◆ **UNDERSTANDING WORD GROUPS**

**Read each group of words. One word in each group doesn't belong.
Find the word and cross it out.**

grenade		Olympics		hospital		worried
~~fisherman~~		medal		accident		sorry
army		champion		school		depressed
soldier		letter		doctors		excited

◆ **FINDING INFORMATION**

Read each question. Find the answer in the paragraph below and circle it. Write the number of the question above your answer.

1. Why were there no Olympic Games in 1940 and 1944?
2. How many years did Takács practice for the Olympics?
3. Where did he go in 1948?
4. Who went with him?
5. What did he win there?
6. When did he return to the Olympics?

In 1940 and 1944, there were no Olympic Games *1* (because of World War II). So Károly had eight years to practice. In 1948, he went to the Olympics with the Hungarian team. He won the gold medal in pistol shooting. In 1952, he returned to the Olympics and won another gold medal in pistol shooting.

◆ **UNDERSTANDING SEQUENCE**

When did it happen? Match the dates and the sentences. Write your answer on the line.

▶ He won his second Olympic gold medal.

▶ He practiced for the Olympics.

▶ Takács lost his right hand in a grenade accident.

▶ He won his first Olympic gold medal.

▶ He won the Hungarian National Pistol-Shooting Competition.

1938	*Takács lost his right hand in a grenade accident.*
1939	_____
1940–1948	_____
1948	_____
1952	_____

4. WRITING/DISCUSSION

Károly Takács is a national hero in Hungary. Who is a national hero in your native country?

A. Complete the sentence. Here, for example, is what one student wrote.

Juan Santamaría is a national hero in _____*Costa Rica*_____ because *he set fire to a hacienda during a battle, and he helped the Costa Rican people win a war* .

_____ is a national hero in _____ because

_____

_____.

B. Read your sentence to the class. If you can, tell the class more about the national hero.

1. PRE-READING

Look at the picture.

▶ Four of the people in the photo are from Vietnam. What do you know about Vietnam? Tell the class.

▶ Can you guess how the people feel?

Read the title of the story. Look at the picture again.

▶ What do you think this story is about?

▶ Can you guess what happens?

The Bottle

In 1979 Dorothy and John Peckham, a Los Angeles couple, went to Hawaii on vacation. They traveled by ship.

Some people on the ship were throwing bottles into the ocean. Each bottle had a piece of paper in it. On each piece of paper were a name, an address, and a message: "If you find this bottle, write to us."

Mrs. Peckham wanted to throw a bottle into the ocean, too. She wrote her name and address on a piece of paper. She put the piece of paper and $1 into a bottle. She put a cap on the bottle and threw the bottle into the water.

Three years later and 9,000 miles[1] away, Hoa Van Nguyen was on a boat, too. But Mr. Nguyen was not on vacation. He was a refugee from Vietnam. Mr. Nguyen, his brother, and 30 other people were going to Thailand in a small boat. The boat was in the Gulf of Thailand.

There wasn't any drinking water in the boat, and Hoa was thirsty. He saw a bottle in the sea. The bottle was floating near the boat. "What's in the bottle? Maybe it's drinking water," he thought. Hoa took the bottle out of the sea and opened it. There wasn't any water in the bottle. But there was a dollar bill and a piece of paper. A name and an address were on the paper. The name was Peckham. The address was in Los Angeles, California.

Hoa and his brother arrived at the refugee camp in Thailand. Hoa used the dollar to buy some stamps. Then he wrote a letter to Mrs. Peckham. "We received a floating mailbox by a bottle on the way from Vietnam to Thailand," Hoa wrote. "Now we send a letter to the boss and we wish you will answer us."

Hoa's English was not perfect, but Mrs. Peckham understood it. She answered Hoa's letter. Hoa wrote another letter and she answered it, too. For two years, Hoa and Mrs. Peckham wrote back and forth. When Hoa got married at the camp, the Peckhams congratulated him. When Hoa and his wife had a baby boy, the Peckhams sent them money. Finally Hoa asked the Peckhams, "Will you help me and my family? We want to come to the United States."

In 1985 the Nguyen family—Hoa, his wife, their son, and Hoa's brother—arrived in Los Angeles. Dorothy and John Peckham were waiting for them at the airport. When the Nguyens and the Peckhams met, they all began to cry. Their tears were tears of happiness.

A few months after the Nguyens came to the United States, Mrs. Nguyen had another baby—a baby girl. The Nguyens named their daughter Dorothy.

[1] 15,000 kilometers

2. VOCABULARY

Complete the sentences with the words below.

floating	refugee	tears

1. Hoa Van Nguyen couldn't stay in Vietnam because it was dangerous for him there. He went to Thailand as a _____refugee_____.

2. Hoa saw a bottle on top of the water. It was _____ near the boat.

3. The Peckhams and the Nguyens cried at the airport. They cried _____ of happiness.

3. COMPREHENSION

◆ FINDING INFORMATION

What information is in the story? What information is not in the story?

There are two correct ways to complete each sentence. Circle the letters of the *two* correct answers.

1. Dorothy and John Peckham
   a. went to Hawaii on vacation.
   b. traveled by ship.
   c. traveled first class.

2. Mrs. Peckham threw a bottle into the ocean. In the bottle, she put
   a. a coin for good luck.
   b. a piece of paper.
   c. a dollar.

3. When Hoa Van Nguyen found Mrs. Peckham's bottle,
   a. it was three years later.
   b. he was 29 years old.
   c. he was in a boat in the Gulf of Thailand.

4. When Hoa arrived at the refugee camp in Thailand, he
   a. bought some stamps.
   b. wrote a letter to Mrs. Peckham.
   c. slept for 13 hours.

5. At the refugee camp, Hoa
   a. got married.
   b. learned English.
   c. became the father of a boy.

6. When the Nguyens arrived in Los Angeles,
   a. the Peckhams were waiting for them.
   b. the Nguyens and the Peckhams cried.
   c. it was 2 A.M.

◆ UNDERSTANDING A SUMMARY

Imagine this: You want to tell the story "The Bottle" to a friend. You want to tell the story quickly, in only four sentences. Which four sentences tell the story best? Check (✓) your answer.

☐ 1. Dorothy Peckham wrote her name and address on a piece of paper, put the paper into a bottle, and threw the bottle into the ocean. The bottle floated to the Gulf of Thailand, 9,000 miles away. Hoa Van Nguyen, a refugee from Vietnam, found the bottle. He opened it because he was thirsty and thought, "Maybe there's drinking water in this bottle."

☐ 2. Dorothy Peckham wrote her name and address on a piece of paper, put the paper into a bottle, and threw the bottle into the ocean. The bottle floated to the Gulf of Thailand, 9,000 miles away. Hoa Van Nguyen, a refugee from Vietnam, found the bottle and wrote to Mrs. Peckham. She helped Mr. Nguyen and his family come to the United States.

Read each group of words. One word or phrase in each group doesn't belong. Find it and cross it out.

letter	Vietnam	in 1979	boss
stamps	Thailand	at the airport	son
mailbox	Los Angeles	in 1985	daughter
~~refugee~~	United States	three months later	brother

4. DISCUSSION

The dotted line on the map shows the way the Nguyens came to the United States. On the same map, draw the way you came to the United States.

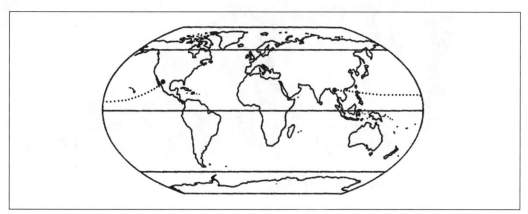

Show your map to a partner. Tell your partner about your trip to the United States.

5. WRITING

Are you living in the United States? Read about the Nguyens' trip to the United States. Then write about your trip on your own paper.

1. The Nguyens came to the United States because they didn't like the government in Vietnam. Why did you come to the United States?
   I came to the United States because . . .

2. The Nguyens came to the United States on April 23, 1985. When did you come?

3. The Nguyens came by airplane. How did you come?

4. The Nguyens' trip was 15 hours long. How long was your trip?

5. The Nguyens arrived in Los Angeles. Where did you arrive?

6. The Nguyens felt tired but happy. How did you feel?

UNIT 21

1. PRE-READING

Look at the picture.

▸ What words can you read on the box?

▸ Do you know who Yoda is? If you know, tell the class.

▸ Can you guess how the woman feels?

Read the title of the story. Look at the picture again.

▸ What do you think this story is about?

▸ Can you guess what happens?

The Last Laugh

Jodee Berry was a waitress at a big restaurant in Florida. One day the restaurant's manager told the waitresses he had exciting news. "In May we're going to have a contest at the restaurant," he said. "The waitress who sells the most food and drinks will win a new Toyota. So try to sell a lot of food and a lot of drinks during the month of May."

"Are you serious?" the waitresses asked the manager. "The top waitress will get a car?"

"A new Toyota," the manager repeated. "So work really hard in May. At the end of the month, one of you will have a new Toyota."

Jodee was excited about the contest. She was a good waitress and a hard worker. "I can win that contest," she thought.

During the month of May, Jodee worked extra hard. She sold a lot of food and drinks. At the end of the month, the manager announced the winner of the contest. It was Jodee! Jodee was very excited. "Now I'll get my new Toyota," she thought.

The manager covered Jodee's eyes with a blindfold and led her to the restaurant's parking lot. Then he uncovered her eyes. Jodee looked around the parking lot. She didn't see a new Toyota.

"Where's my Toyota?" she asked the manager.

The manager gave Jodee a box. "Here it is!" the manager said. "Here's your new toy Yoda!" The manager laughed.

At first, Jodee didn't understand. She looked at the box. Inside the box, there was a green doll. It was Yoda, a character from the *Star Wars* movies.

"Get it?" the manager asked. "It's a joke. You thought I said, 'Toyota.' But I said, 'Toy Yoda.' So here it is: your new toy Yoda." The manager laughed again.

Jodee didn't laugh. She was furious.

The next week, Jodee quit her job at the restaurant. Then she went to court. She told a judge her story. The manager told the judge his story, too. The judge listened to both stories and made a decision: The manager had to buy Jodee a new car.

"Go to a Toyota dealer," the judge told Jodee, "and pick out a new Toyota. The manager will pay for it."

"Any Toyota?" Jodee asked the judge.

"Any Toyota," the judge answered.

The next day, Jodee was driving a shiny new Toyota. Now it was her turn to laugh.

2. VOCABULARY

Which words have the same meaning as the words in *italics*? Write the letter of your answer on the line.

_b_ **1.** The manager *said again,* "A new Toyota."

_____ **2.** Jodee was the *best* waitress.

_____ **3.** "*Do you understand*?" the manager asked. "It's a joke."

_____ **4.** Jodee was *very angry.*

_____ **5.** She *stopped working* at the restaurant.

a. furious

b. repeated

c. quit her job

d. top

e. Get it?

3. PRACTICING PRONUNCIATION

The underlined words are in the story. If you can say them correctly, you can say the words below them correctly, too. Practice with your teacher.

had	will	new	get	repeat	lot	drink
bad	bill	blew	let	beat	hot	blink
dad	fill	flew	met	heat	not	pink
mad	hill	grew	pet	neat	pot	sink
sad	Jill	stew	wet	seat	spot	stink

4. COMPREHENSION

◆ REVIEWING THE STORY

Complete each sentence. Then read the story again and check your answers.

Jodee Berry was a _____*waitress*_____ at a big restaurant. The manager
said, "We're going to have a _____ at the restaurant. The top
waitress will _____ a new Toyota."

Jodee worked extra _____ and won the contest. But the
manager didn't give her a car. He gave her a green doll. It was Yoda, a
character in the *Star Wars* _____.

Jodee went to court. The _____ decided that the manager
had to buy Jodee a new Toyota.

◆ FINDING MORE INFORMATION

Read each sentence on the left. Which sentence on the right gives you more information? Write the letter of your answer on the line.

1. The manager had exciting news. _d_

2. Jodee worked extra hard. ____

3. The manager announced the winner of the contest. ____

4. Inside the box, there was a green doll. ____

5. The judge made a decision. ____

a. She sold a lot of food and drinks.

b. It was Jodee.

c. The manager had to buy Jodee a new car.

d. He said, "We're going to have a contest at the restaurant."

e. It was Yoda, a character from the *Star Wars* movies.

5. WRITING/DISCUSSION

Jodee was a waitress. What about you? What kind of work do you do?

A. In the spaces below, draw three pictures. In the first space, draw the work you did in your native country. In the second space, draw the work you do now. In the third space, draw the work you want to do. When you finish drawing, complete the sentences.

my work before   my work now

the work I want

1. In my country, I worked as a/an _____.

2. Now I work as a/an _____.

3. I want to work as a/an _____.

B. Share your drawings and your sentences with the class.

UNIT 22

1. PRE-READING

Look at the picture on the right.

▶ Where are the men from?

▶ How old are they?

▶ Can you guess how they feel?

Read the title of the story. Look at the picture again.

▶ What do you think this story is about?

▶ Can you guess what happens?

Old Friends

Chi Hsii, an 11-year-old boy, hurried along the road from his village in China. He carried a basket of eggs.

U.S. soldiers were at a camp near the boy's village. They were standing around a fire. When they saw the Chinese boy, they said, "Here comes breakfast."

It was November 1945. World War II was over. There was no more fighting. But there wasn't much food in China. Every day the Chinese boy brought some eggs to the U.S. soldiers. The soldiers took the eggs and gave the boy canned food. The soldiers were happy; they had fresh eggs. And the boy was happy; he had canned food.

Day after day, the Chinese boy traded food with the soldiers. The Chinese boy liked the soldiers, and the soldiers liked the Chinese boy. But there was a problem. The American soldiers couldn't say the boy's name. They tried and they tried, but they couldn't say "Chi Hsii." "Chi Hsii" sounds a little like the English words "two shoes." So, the soldiers called the boy "Charlie Two Shoes."

One day Charlie's father came with Charlie to the soldiers' camp. "We don't have enough food in our village," he said. "Please take my son. Take good care of him." For the next three years, Charlie Two Shoes lived with the American soldiers in their camp. He ate with the soldiers and dressed like the soldiers. He learned to read and write English at an American school.

In 1949 the soldiers left China. They flew back to the United States. They couldn't take Charlie with them. From the windows of the airplane, the soldiers looked at Charlie. Charlie was crying. The soldiers were crying, too.

After the soldiers left, they often thought about Charlie. They were afraid that Charlie was dead. Then, in 1980, they got a letter from Charlie. Charlie was alive! He wanted to come to the United States.

The soldiers sent Charlie a plane ticket. Charlie came to the United States and lived with one of the soldiers. Later the soldiers bought plane tickets for Charlie's wife and three children, too. They also gave Charlie $5,000 to open a Chinese restaurant.

Sometimes people ask the soldiers, "Why did you give Charlie so much help?" The soldiers answer, "We were unhappy in China; we were cold and lonely. Then came Charlie. He was always smiling, always happy. When Charlie was with us, we felt happy. Yes, we gave a lot to Charlie. But Charlie gave a lot to us, too."

2. VOCABULARY

Complete the sentences with the words below.

camp	over	traded	village

1. The soldiers' houses had no bathrooms, kitchens, or heat. The soldiers built fires to keep warm. They cooked over the fires, too. The soldiers lived in a

   _____*camp*_____ .

2. Chi Hsii's town in China was very small. He lived in a _____ .

3. In November 1945, the fighting was finished. World War II was _____ .

4. The Chinese boy gave the soldiers eggs, and the soldiers gave the boy canned food. The Chinese boy _____ food with the soldiers.

3. COMPREHENSION

◆ **REMEMBERING DETAILS**

One word in each sentence is not correct. Find the word and cross it out. Write the correct word.

1. Chi Hsii was a ~~French~~ *Chinese* boy.

2. U.S. doctors were at a camp near the boy's village.

3. World War I was over.

4. Every day the Chinese boy brought some fruit to the U.S. soldiers.

5. Chi Hsii sounds a little like the Spanish words "two shoes."

6. For the next three days, Charlie Two Shoes lived with the American soldiers in their camp.

7. In 1949 the soldiers flew back to England.

8. After the soldiers left, they never thought about Charlie.

◆ **UNDERSTANDING CAUSE AND EFFECT**

Find the best way to complete each sentence. Write the letter of your answer on the line.

1. When the soldiers saw the Chinese boy, they said, "Here comes breakfast" __b__

2. The American soldiers called the boy "Charlie Two Shoes" ____

3. All the soldiers were sad ____

4. The soldiers gave a lot to Charlie ____

a. because they couldn't say "Chi Hsii."

b. because he brought them eggs every day.

c. because Charlie gave a lot to them.

d. because they couldn't take Charlie with them to the United States.

◆ **UNDERSTANDING A SUMMARY**

Imagine this: You want to tell the story "Old Friends" to *your* friend. You want to tell the story quickly, in only four sentences. Which four sentences tell the story best? Check (✓) your answer.

☐ 1. After World War II, a Chinese boy lived with U.S. soldiers in their camp in China. The soldiers called the boy "Charlie Two Shoes" because they couldn't say his Chinese name. When the soldiers went back to the U.S., they couldn't take Charlie with them. Thirty-one years later, the soldiers helped Charlie and his family come to the U.S.

☐ 2. After World War II, there were U.S. soldiers in China. Some soldiers lived in a camp near a Chinese village. Every day a Chinese boy from the village brought eggs to the U.S. soldiers, and the soldiers gave the boy canned food. The soldiers were happy because they had fresh eggs, and the boy was happy because he had canned food.

4. WRITING / DISCUSSION

Charlie's old friends gave him $5,000 to open a Chinese restaurant. Imagine this: Someone gives your class money to open an international restaurant. What dish from your country will be on the menu?

A. On your own paper, draw a picture of the dish. Then answer the questions below. Show your picture to a partner. Tell your partner about the dish from your native country.

1. What is the name of the dish? _____

2. What is it made of? _____

3. Who makes this dish in your family? _____

4. When do you eat it? (For example, "We eat it in the summer" or "We eat it only on holidays.") _____

B. Charlie and the soldiers were old friends. On your own paper, draw a picture of an old friend. Then complete the sentences below. Show your picture to a partner. Tell your partner about your old friend.

1. My friend's name is _____.

2. I met my friend in _____.

3. My friend lives in _____.

4. He/She is _____.

5. Together we _____.

6. I like my friend because _____.

To the Teacher

The original newspaper and magazine versions of these TRUE STORIES contain information that could not be included in the adaptations. Sometimes the information was too complicated to include; sometimes including it would have made the stories too long for the allotted space. On the other hand, the information—in many cases, the story behind the story—was just too interesting to leave out entirely. So, it was decided that additional facts and updates would be given here, in a special "To the Teacher" section.

As you will see from the sophistication of the language, this section is not meant to be read by students. You might want to offer the information only if students seem puzzled or curious, or if, in the context of the class discussion, the information would be particularly meaningful.

Also included here are supplemental reading and vocabulary activities, all of them no-prep, as well as specific teaching tips for the discussion and writing exercises.

All Units

Before Reading

A. Illustrate the story.

If your students need extra support, you might want to tell them the story before they read it, stopping well short of the ending. As you tell the story, draw pictures on the board to illustrate it. Following are some tips for drawing.

1. Keep it simple! To draw a person, most of the time just drawing the head and shoulders suffices—no need to draw arms, legs, feet, ears. A few squiggles to represent hair indicates the person is female; no squiggles indicates a male. Smaller heads and shoulders are children. Add two dots for the eyes, a dot for the nose, and a line for the mouth, and the figure is complete.

For example, the figures might look something like these:

2. Use the same symbols consistently to represent the same things so that students get used to your drawing style. For example, two parallel lines with a triangle-shaped roof (resembling a child's drawing of a house) represent a building. A dollar sign inside means the building is a bank; a shopping cart indicates it is a supermarket.

3. Draw nouns to represent verbs. For example, draw a knife to represent "to cut."

4. Feel free to move back and forth between drawing images from the story and acting out scenes. You could even pretend to pick up items you drew on the board (such as a bottle) and use them as props in your reenactment of a scene. Or you could interact with objects you drew. For example, you could knock on a picture of a door.

Drawing tips 1–3 are the suggestions of Norma Shapiro, whose reference book *Chalk Talks* (Command Performance Language Institute, 1994) has further tips and hundreds of examples of simple drawings.

B. Invent a story.

Instead of telling students the actual story, you can guide them into fabricating an alternate version of it by asking questions and encouraging students to guess the answers. Here, for example, is how a pre-reading question-and-answer session for the story "Love or Baseball?" (Unit 10) might play out:

Teacher (pointing to photo of Joe):	What's his name?
Student:	His name is Ramón.
Teacher:	OK, his name is Ramón. What's his last name?
Student:	His last name is Martínez.
Teacher:	OK, his last name is Martínez. What's his favorite sport?
Student:	It's baseball.
Teacher:	OK, his favorite sport is baseball. Ramón wants to watch an important baseball game on TV. When is the game? On Monday? On Friday?
Student:	It's on Sunday.
Teacher:	OK, it's on Sunday. Poor Ramón! He wants to watch the game, but he can't. Why not?
Student:	His TV is broken.
Teacher:	OK, his TV is broken. What does he do?
Students:	He fixes his TV. / He buys a new TV. / He watches the game at his brother's house.
Teacher:	OK, maybe he fixes his TV, maybe he buys a new TV, or maybe he watches the game at his brother's house. [*At this point, the teacher recounts the fabricated story*.] That's *our* story. Now let's read the *true* story.

Students can answer the questions orally, with volunteers guessing answers, or they can write their answers and then read them to a partner. If you choose to make this activity a whole-class effort, you can illustrate the students' answers with simple drawings on the board. (Please see drawing tips on page 90.) After reading, you can go back to the illustrations of the fabricated story and contrast the guessed answers with the actual facts. ("We said his name was Ramón, but his name is . . .")

C. Discuss first.

If you think students might have had experiences similar to those in the story, you might have them complete the discussion exercise before, rather than after, they read. For example, before reading "A Little Traveler" (Unit 7), students could share their experiences of being lost as a child.

D. Pose pre-reading questions.

If your students are comfortable speaking English, you may wish to guide them into posing their own pre-reading questions. After the class describes the photo and reads the title of the story, ask, "What do you want to know?" Write the students' questions on the board. Return to the questions after reading the story to see which were answered.

During Reading

A. Read aloud.

If your students understand spoken English well but have little experience reading, you may wish to begin by reading the story aloud, perhaps stopping short of the last few paragraphs if the story has a surprise ending.

B. Predict the text.

If you are reading the story aloud to students, pause occasionally and ask them, "What will happen next?"

C. Read twice.

Students who have a tendency to stop at every unknown word should be encouraged to read the story twice, once without stopping to get the gist of the story, and then a second time, stopping to underline new vocabulary.

After Reading

A. Read with mistakes.

Read the story aloud, making mistakes as you read. For example, you could begin the story "The Runner" (Unit 3) this way: "One morning a man was *walking* to work when he saw something unusual: *A young* woman was running along the street." Students call out the errors.

B. Whisper read.

Read the story aloud. Students read along with you, mouthing the words inaudibly and trying to keep up with your pace.

C. Stand up when you hear your word.

Write key words from the story on index cards and pass the cards out to selected students. Read the story aloud. Students stand up when they hear the words on their cards. (Because students are continually standing up and sitting down, this is sometimes called a "popcorn" activity. It is especially suitable for young learners.)

D. Rewrite the story.

If students have solid writing skills, they can rewrite the story from a different point of view. For example, the story "Together Again" (Unit 14) could be told by Orestes, his wife, or his son Alejandro as a first-person account.

E. Role-play.

Students write a short skit based on the story and then act out their roles in front of the class. For example, students could act out the conversation between Mrs. Krohn and the police officer (Unit 3), or they could role-play a possible conversation between Joe and his girlfriend (Unit 10) after she sees him at the store without his wheelchair and bandage.

F. Write a walking dictation.

Many units have a Remembering Details exercise in which students find the incorrect word in each sentence, cross it out, and write the correct word. These sentences can be the basis of a "walking dictation." Students place their books on the opposite side of the room. They memorize the first sentence, "carry" it back to their desks, and write it down. They continue walking back and forth until they have copied all the sentences. Then they take their seats, find the incorrect word in each sentence, cross it out, and write the correct word.

G. Write a disappearing summary.

Students, working as a class, summarize the story. (Stipulate that the summary should consist of four or five sentences.) You write their summary on the board, correcting errors as you write or after the summary is complete. Read the first sentence of the summary; students repeat in unison. Erase a word or two of the sentence and say it again; students repeat in unison. Continue erasing words a few at a time. After each erasure, say the sentence and ask students to repeat. Ultimately, students will be saying a sentence that is totally erased. Repeat the process with the remaining sentences. When all the sentences have been erased, ask students to recite the summary from memory. (Pointing to the places on the board where the words were sometimes facilitates recall if students falter.)

All Units

Vocabulary

Research indicates that students' retention of new vocabulary depends not so much on the type of vocabulary exercises they complete but on how much exposure they have to the new words. The more times they "touch" a word, the more likely it is that they will remember it. So you will probably want to follow up the exercises in the text with supplemental activities, such as writing the words on flash cards and presenting them again in subsequent classes. Similarly, research shows that the particular method students use to learn vocabulary—whether they write the new words on small flash cards, for example, or in a vocabulary notebook—is not as important as simply having a system for memorizing vocabulary. So you might present several strategies for learning new words and encourage students to share their own techniques. Knowledge of vocabulary is a key component of reading comprehension, so it is important to devise a system for learning new words in class and to encourage students to devise their own systems for learning words at home.

If your students are employed adults who have little time to study outside of class, it is particularly important to devote some class time to vocabulary study. Following is an effective, no-prep way to review vocabulary in class:

1. Select 8–10 words from the story and, at the end of class or in a subsequent class, write them on the board in random order, perhaps scattering the words across the board.

2. Choose a word and orally describe a situation in which it could be used, but do not say the word. For example, if the target word is *delivered*, from Unit 4, you might say, "Every day the mail carrier gave Ming-fu's letter to Lee. He _____ the letter to her." (Replace the word with a spoken "beep.") The context can be from the story, or it can be a new context—for example: "I went to a store and bought a refrigerator. Some men brought the refrigerator to my house in a truck. They _____ it yesterday." After students call out the target word, draw a line through it. Continue giving examples and drawing lines through the remaining words.

3. When students become comfortable with the activity, student volunteers can take turns giving examples of the target words in context. (You will need to remind them not to say the target words.) Initially, they might balk, but with time they will become skilled at giving examples, sometimes from their own lives.

Unit 1 Dish Soap for Dinner

Lever Brothers, the manufacturer of Sun Light dishwashing liquid, mailed out 52 million free samples of its new product over a two-year time period in the early 1980s. The National Poison Control Center began to notice that calls to local poison control centers came in clusters and that those clusters coincided with regional mailings of samples of Sun Light. The most dramatic evidence of cause and effect occurred on the East Coast of the United States: After 20 million samples were sent to homes there, poison control hot lines lit up with calls from people suffering from diarrhea and vomiting. By the time the correlation between calls to poison control centers and mailings of the soap became evident, the promotion had ended. According to *Newsweek*, approximately 1,000 people ate the soap.

The picture of two lemons remains on bottles of Sun Light; however, the words "with Real Lemon Juice" have been replaced with the words "with Citrus Burst."

Teaching Tip

Many teachers like to introduce this story by passing around a bottle of lemon-scented dishwashing liquid. Ask students to look at the label and sniff the bottle. Then ask, "What is this for?" After they answer, "For washing dishes," ask them, "Is it for putting on salad?" Tell them, "The man in the story put soap on his salad and ate it. Why?"

If you think the concept of a "free sample" might be problematic, you could bring in some actual free samples (or trial-size products to represent free samples), or you could tell a story like the following: "Yesterday I went to the supermarket. A woman was giving people small pieces of pizza. 'Would you like one?' she asked me. I asked her, 'How much is it?' She said, 'It's free. Try it.' It was a free sample."

The discussion exercise asks students to share stories of mistakes they made. Initially, students might be reluctant to share their stories. If you have a story about a mistake you made while traveling or living in another country, begin the discussion by telling the story. That often gets the ball rolling. Also encourage students to share strategies they use so they don't make mistakes (always carrying a map, for instance).

Unit 2 A New Man

Roley McIntyre was chosen "Slimmer of the Year" by a British reducing magazine. Before he lost two-thirds of his body weight, Mr. McIntyre was wider than he was tall (height 5'10"; girth 6'6").

Teaching Tip

Teacher Anjie Martin, Whitewater (Wisconsin) Community Education, suggests an alternate writing / discussion exercise. Students make two lists under the headings: "Food I Like That's Good for Me" and "Food I Like That's Not Good for Me." They compare their lists with a partner's or contribute a few items on their lists to master lists on the board. The activity can foster a sense of community when students discover they share a taste for many of the same "good" and "bad" foods.

Unit 3 The Runner

Sigrid Krohn de Lange was running through the streets of Bergen, Norway. In an interview with a Norwegian radio station, she described her experience with the Bergen police. The *True Stories* version of the story is based on her first-person account, which is as follows: "They thought I had escaped from a nursing home. A motorist had called the police to say there was a strange lady running. The police officer could not believe that such an old lady could be out jogging. I said there was nothing wrong with my head nor my legs.

He had to check that I lived at the address I gave him. When that was clear, I could continue my jogging." A photo of Mrs. Krohn was not available, so a model posed for the photo that accompanies the story. The model is an avid walker and bicyclist who routinely rides her bicycle 21 miles at a stretch. She is only 86 years old.

Teaching Tip

An alternate writing / discussion exercise might be asking the class to work as a group to generate a list of things old people do in their native countries. In a multicultural class, the resulting list might illuminate some cultural similarities and differences.

An appropriate follow-up to this unit is a lesson on giving personal information (phone number, address, etc.).

Unit 4 The Love Letters

Several sources credit United Press International (UPI) for this tale of unrequited love. It dates from the 1970s. UPI computerized files do not go back that far, so the *True Stories* version could not be adapted from primary sources. The story is, however, true; the UPI reporter in Taipei at that time recalls writing it.

It is not known if Lee and the mail carrier lived happily ever after.

Teaching Tip

In the discussion exercise, men and women vote separately on the best ideas for Ming-fu. When the males' and females' top choices differ, a spirited discussion can ensue. If you teach adults, you can further personalize the discussion by asking the married men how they won their wives' love and the married women how their husbands won their love.

If your students have the oral skills to work independently in small groups, you can turn the discussion exercise into a small-group activity. Students work in small groups until they agree on the five best ideas and then report their choices to the class.

Unit 5   Bad Luck, Good Luck

Vegard's name is pronounced VEH-gard. His last name is actually Sjaastad, which was changed to the more easily pronounced name Olsen for the story. He lives in the western Norwegian town of Aalesund.

In Norway, all Visa cards have the owner's photo embossed on the back. When the thief presented the card to Vegard, he gave it to him photo side up. "It was like I met myself in the doorway," Vegard said in an interview with the Associated Press. The thief did not seem to recognize Vegard from the picture. Vegard said, "I wasn't going to play hero. I'm pretty calm by nature. I just accepted the card and said, 'I hope you enjoy the meal.'" When the police went to the thief's house, they found not only Vegard's wallet and music CDs but also other goods they suspected were stolen.

Teaching Tip

This story affords an opportunity to discuss identity theft. Many websites give tips for preventing identity theft, including steps to take if an I.D. has been stolen. The story also invites a discussion of the pros and cons of credit cards. You might begin the discussion by making two headings on the board: "Credit cards are good because . . ." and "Credit cards are bad because . . . ." Students supply possible ways to complete the sentences.

Unit 6   Lost and Found

The triplets had more in common than their appearance: They all liked Italian food, soft rock music, wrestling, and the same brand of cigarettes. In an interview with *Good Housekeeping* magazine, each triplet reported having recurrent dreams in which he had a brother who looked just like him.

According to *Newsday*, the triplets may have been separated at birth because a psychiatrist advising the adoption agency thought it was best for them to grow up apart; that way, each could develop his own personality and not have to compete for his parents' attention. Now the opposite is believed to be true: Multiples should be raised together. Adoption agencies no longer separate multiple-birth children; the triplets were probably the last such infants separated at birth.

Described as "natural clowns," the brothers were popular guests on TV talk shows in the months after their 1980 reunion. Eight years later, they teamed up to open a successful restaurant (called Triplets) in New York City. Bob Shafran later left the restaurant business to enter law school. Eddy Galland died in 1995.

Unit 7   A Little Traveler

The Cabrera farm is just outside the border city of Tecate, Mexico. Tomás was found in California, about 70 miles east of San Diego. He had been missing for 30 hours.

Teaching Tip

The writing exercise asks students to write about the experience of being lost as a child. Most students have memories of being lost as a child, at least for a few minutes, or know someone who was. However, if there are students who have not had that experience, you can modify the exercise. First, identify the students who have a story to tell about being lost. (The story can be about themselves, or it can be about a friend or relative.) Students without such an experience interview those students, using the questions in the text to guide them. They write their classmate's answers and then tell the class about the classmate's experience. (Note that if the experience was not the student's, but someone else's, the interviewer will need to alter the questions. For example, question 1 would not be "How old were you?" but "How old was he/she?").

Unit 8   Man's Best Friend

Bobby is known as "Greyfriars Bobby" because he kept his 14-year vigil in the graveyard of historic Greyfriars Church in Edinburgh. The stone on Bobby's grave reads: "Died January 14, 1872, aged 16 years. His loyalty and devotion were an object lesson to us all."

Unit 9 The Coin

The *Illawarra Mercury* reported that the coin—a 1959 Australian threepence—was lodged between Marie's vocal chords and prevented them from vibrating. The coin wasn't spotted on the x-ray because it was thin and resting in a horizontal position. Marie's mother no longer puts coins in her Christmas cake.

Abbie Tom, a teacher at Durham Technical College in North Carolina, reports that she asked her students how they thought Marie felt during all those years when she couldn't talk. An elderly Russian said, "Just like us. We can't talk either."

Unit 10 Love or Baseball?

It was actually one of his girlfriend's friends, not the girlfriend herself, who spotted Joe walking through a local store without his bandage. Joe told the *MetroWest Daily*, "I didn't even know I'd got caught until she called me later that night."

"How's your broken leg?" his girlfriend asked. "It's healing," Joe replied. She asked him why her friend had seen him walking through the store. The truth came out, and the relationship ended minutes later. "A stupid baseball game means more to you than me," Joe's girlfriend said before she hung up the phone.

Joe said he was disappointed the romance ended because he "kind of liked the girl," whom he'd dated for five months. Still, he didn't regret his decision to choose the game over the girl. "Girlfriends come and go," he said, "but you only get one chance to see the game that sent the New York Yankees to the World Series."

Teaching Tip

You might ask the students to suggest other solutions to Joe's dilemma, perhaps phrasing the question this way: "Joe doesn't want to go to the dance. He wants to watch the baseball game. What can he do?"

In the writing / discussion exercise, students circulate throughout the room looking for people who share their interests. Beginning-level students who participated in field-testing this activity spontaneously came up with the question they needed to ask ("Do you like to _____?"). However, once they found classmates with matching interests, they had trouble spelling their names. So, before students circulate, you might want to review the question "How do you spell your name?"

Unit 11 Buried Alive

The people who could verify Max Hoffman's story—his parents, the neighbor, the doctor—are no longer alive. Also gone are the friends and neighbors who knew Mr. Hoffman in Clinton, Iowa, and could perhaps vouch for his honesty. Max Hoffman's story survives in the form of a three-page autobiography that he dictated to a friend. That autobiography, as well as a photo of Max Hoffman (unfortunately too blurry to be included in this book), is in the hands of Iowans Edward Ridyard and William Rolston, who believe the story is true.

It is said that Max Hoffman kept the silver handles from his small coffin as a memento and carried them with him everywhere. Where are the silver handles now? They were buried with Max Hoffman in 1953.

Teaching Tip

Many teachers use this story around the time of Halloween. Jonathan Tegnell, who teaches at a high school in Saitama, Japan, reports success with this follow-up activity: "I asked the students to each silently think of a famous dead person. While they did this, I brought a desk to the front, lit a candle on it, lowered the lights, and put on some spooky music. I demonstrated the activity first. We were to imagine that the ghost of our famous dead person was inhabiting us, but this ghost could answer only 'yes' or 'no.' To guarantee that only *yes / no* questions would be asked, I made *yes / no* paddles out of cardboard and disposable chopsticks. (They were shaped like skulls with bone-font lettering.)

Students were to try to figure out who the ghost was. Obviously this was just a glorified version of the game Twenty Questions, but it was quite successful. It encouraged creative, communicative use of language while forcing students to do so within limited formal constraints. In addition, they really enjoyed it, which is the main thing that made it successful."

Unit 12 The Winning Ticket

When the woman scratched off the pictures on her lottery ticket, she saw $25,000, another $25,000, and a gold nugget. The gold nugget functioned as a wild card, meaning the woman won the $50,000 "instant prize." She threw the ticket on the counter because she assumed she needed three of a kind to win.

Ms. Costabile was a college student who worked part time at the drugstore. She told the *San Jose Mercury News* that she never considered keeping the ticket. "I don't think I would have felt good, knowing it was somebody else's ticket," she said.

Unit 13 Thank You

In the story, the lines wrapped around the whale's body are described as "fishing lines." They were actually crab-trap lines—nylon ropes that link crab traps. Each rope is about 240 feet long, with weights every 60 feet. The whale had about 20 of these lines wrapped around its body. As the whale struggled to free itself, the lines became tighter and made visible cuts in its blubber. In addition, at least 12 crab traps were hanging from the whale. Each trap weighed 90 pounds, and the weight of the traps was pulling the whale down, making it difficult for it to keep its blowhole out of the water.

Did the whale really return to say "thank you"? The *San Francisco Chronicle* reported: "Whale experts say it's nice to think that the whale was thanking its rescuers, but nobody really knows what was on its mind." Still, the divers who freed the whale believed that it was expressing gratitude. "It felt to me like it was thanking us, knowing that it was free and that we had helped it," one diver said. "I never felt threatened. It was an amazing, incredible experience." The man who witnessed the rescue from the boat added, "You hate to anthropomorphize too much, but the whale was doing little dives and the guys were rubbing shoulders with it. I don't know for sure what it was thinking, but it's something that I will always remember. It was just too cool."

Teaching Tip

Male humpback whales sing the longest and most complex songs in the animal kingdom. On the website of the American Cetacean Society (and on other websites as well), students can listen to recordings of their songs.

Unit 14 Together Again

In a 1999 interview with the *New York Post*, Orestes Lorenzo revealed that his decision to defect was not on the spur of the moment. He had become increasingly disillusioned with the Cuban government and was becoming more and more withdrawn at home. When his wife suspected he was having an affair, he had to tell her that he was contemplating leaving Cuba, whispering because he feared that microphones were planted in their home. She whispered back, "Go. Escape."

Once he arrived in the United States, he worked relentlessly to be reunited with his family. He wrote countless letters, appealed to the U.S. Congress, and testified before the United Nations. At one point, he so desperately wanted his sons to grow up in the United States that he offered Castro a deal: He would fly to Cuba and turn himself in if Castro would let his family emigrate to the United States.

When Orestes flew to Cuba to retrieve his family, he intended to land on the beach but overshot it. So he was forced to land on the highway, narrowly avoiding a head-on collision with an oncoming truck. Orestes and the stunned truck driver both slammed on their brakes and stopped within yards of each another—so close that Orestes could see every line on the driver's face. He had 40 seconds to get his family into the plane and take off again before he could be targeted by missiles. "Even I thought the plan was crazy," he told *People* magazine, "but I had to try. I would rather die than leave my family there." When the plane crossed the 24th parallel and left Cuban air space, Orestes turned to his wife and said, "We're together—together forever."

In 2000, Orestes's parents and two brothers, along with their families, immigrated to the United States. The Lorenzo family lives in Orlando, Florida.

Teaching Tip

In the writing / discussion exercise, students make lists of things they like and dislike in the United States and in their native countries. If your students are in their native country, you might ask them about the place where they are living. What do they like about it? What don't they like about it? They make two lists under the headings "Like" and "Don't like" and compare their lists with a partner's. Alternately, you might ask students to imagine that they are going to live in the United States for one year. What do they think they will like? What do they think they won't like? They make two lists under the headings "I will like" and "I won't like" and compare their lists with a partner's.

Unit 15 Saved by the Bell

Newspaper accounts do not mention the fate of Leonardo's climbing companions, so it is assumed they made it down the mountain safely.

Leonardo was a novice climber, and it was his first time on the mountain. When he became separated from his friends in a blizzard, he wasn't worried initially. "Since it was my first climb," he told a reporter from the *Sunday Herald*, "the storm looked beautiful to me and I enjoyed it." It wasn't until the next day that he realized he was in grave danger. By the end of the day, shortly before he was rescued, he could no longer move his extremities.

Representatives from the phone company called Leonardo every half hour while he was waiting for the rescue team. "The calls injected me with human warmth, with strength," he said. During one of the calls, his cell phone battery went dead. Leonardo remembered that when he was a child, he used to extend the life of batteries by putting them in the freezer. So he buried the dead battery in the snow. Half an hour later, it was working again.

When he was safely off the mountain, rescuers called the phone company in Bogota to tell everyone that Leonardo was OK. There was a celebration in the office.

The expression "saved by the bell," incidentally, was originally a boxing term. At the end of a boxing round, a bell is rung. If the bell rings before a knocked-down boxer is counted out, he or she can get up and continue fighting in the next round. It has come to mean "rescued at the last minute."

Teaching Tip

In the discussion exercise, students make a list of supplies to have on hand in case of an emergency. On the website of the Centers for Disease Control (CDC), there are lists of supplies needed for specific disasters— earthquakes, floods, radiation, wildfires. The rule of thumb is that there should be enough supplies to last for three days. In addition, it is recommended that each family have a disaster supply kit that could be taken along with them in case they have to evacuate their home. Here are some items that are common to many lists:

1. First-aid kit (containing hydrogen peroxide, antibiotic ointment, pain medication, diarrhea medicine, bandages, scissors, tweezers, thermometer, instant cold packs for sprains)

2. Three gallons of water for each person (enough for three days)

3. Canned or packaged food (enough for three days)

4. Food and water for pets (enough for three days)

5. Nonelectric can opener

6. Paper cups and plates; plastic eating utensils

7. Pre-moistened towelettes

8. Candles

9. Sturdy shoes

10. Sleeping bags

11. Flashlight

12. Battery-powered radio

13. Extra batteries

14. Tools (screwdriver, pliers, hammer, adjustable wrench)

15. Fire extinguisher

16. Copies of important documents, kept in a waterproof container

Unit 16 This Is the Place for Me

On Walter Polovchak's 18th birthday, the *Chicago Tribune* reported that although Walter and his lawyer "have not exactly beat the system that ruled, alternately, for and against them, they have outlasted it."

In 1980 Walter refused to accompany his parents back to Ukraine, which was then part of the Soviet Union. "Never I go back," he vowed. President Carter granted Walter political asylum. During the ensuing five-year legal battle, Walter's cause was championed by conservative political groups; his parents' efforts were backed by the American Civil Liberties Union. When Walter turned 18, his parents sent him a telegram that read simply, "Best Wishes. Congratulations. We wish you well."

Walter has visited his parents in Ukraine several times. He believes his father regrets his decision to return to Ukraine. In an interview with the *Chicago Sun-Times*, he said, "I think he realizes he made a mistake. He hasn't come out and said it. But in many ways, he regrets going back. He didn't know how things would work out."

For years Walter lived quietly in a Chicago suburb, working as a manager at a shipping and receiving center, but he reentered the limelight during the Elián González controversy in 2000. Elián's mother, who was divorced from his father, drowned trying to come with Elián to the United States from Cuba. She strapped Elián to an inner tube, and he survived. A tug-of-war between Elián's father and his Miami relatives ensued. Walter Polovchak believed strongly that Elián should stay in the United States and that Elián's father and stepmother should join him in Florida. He flew to Miami and energized the supporters who had gathered outside Elián's house with the cry: "Long Live Freedom!" He then went into the house and spoke to Elián. Scott Holleran, a freelance reporter who witnessed the meeting, describes it as follows: "As Polovchak crouched before the child and looked him in the eye, a hush fell over the guests and family, and all eyes were on the world's youngest defector and the child who is the heir to his legacy. Elián, still and serious, listened to the pale stranger. In a solid Chicago accent that bore no trace of the Ukrainian language of his youth, Polovchak told Elián, 'Hang in there, stay strong, and this will end soon. One day, you can come up to Chicago, visit me and my son, and play with him.' "

In a statement he released to the press, Polovchak wrote: "Elián González is faced with one of the most difficult decisions that one can face in life—the choice between freedom and family. I have also faced this decision. Family is extremely important, but for some, the opportunity for freedom comes once in a lifetime. For me, it was one of the hardest decisions I've had to make, and I do not regret it. If I had to do it all over again, I would."

Three weeks later, Elián was taken from his relatives' home by eight armed INS officials and returned to his father in Cuba.

Walter's sister, Natalie, is married, with two children, and also lives in Illinois.

Teaching Tip

To turn the second discussion exercise into a whole-class activity, draw the graph on the board, replacing the drawings in the book with simpler figures: a happy face, a sad face, and a neutral face (with a faint smile). Students come to the board and put an X on the line at the place that reflects the way they feel. More often than not, students will put their X in a predictable place; that is, those who have lived in a new country from six weeks to six months will put their X on the descending line, while students who have been in the new country longer will put their X on the ascending line. This activity reassures students that their feelings reflect normal stages in cultural acclimation and are shared by others in the class. Point out that the ascending line to the "at home" stage is more gradual than the steeper and shorter descending line to the sad state, and remind students that it generally takes a year or two to reach that final stage.

Unit 17 Nicole's Party

Nicole met Tasos, who lived in London, on a beach in Greece, where they were both vacationing. After a whirlwind transatlantic courtship, Tasos gave her a four-carat diamond engagement ring. Nicole was a kindergarten teacher, and at the end of the school year, she resigned her position to devote herself to planning for her November wedding, which cost her father $125,000. "It was supposed to be a fairy-tale wedding," she told the *Daily News*. "Well, it did have a happy ending. There just wasn't a groom."

At the rehearsal dinner the night before the wedding, Tasos had joked, "It's a good thing Nicole has my passport. I'm having second thoughts." Everyone laughed. The first sentence turned out not to be true; Nicole didn't have his passport. But the second

sentence was true; Tasos was indeed having second thoughts. On the day of the wedding, he vanished without a trace. He was later found at a luxury resort in Tahiti, on his honeymoon alone. "I just wanted to get away," he told reporters. Tasos's reasons for backing out of the wedding never became public.

Four years after being jilted, Nicole became engaged to another man. That time, the groom showed up for the wedding.

Unit 18 A Strong Little Boy

Newsweek reported that when Jimmy was pulled from the water, his body temperature was 84 degrees, and he was clinically dead. At the hospital, he was put on a cold mattress and given drugs to induce a coma to reduce the risk that his brain would swell, a potentially lethal complication of near-drowning.

Jimmy is now a healthy adult, six feet tall. However, according to *USA Today*, "his recovery was marred by learning disabilities and his parents' divorce." Doctors who treated Jimmy refuse to speculate on whether the learning disabilities were the result of oxygen deprivation while he was submerged in the water.

Unit 19 The Champion

The story recounts Takács's experience at the Hungarian National Pistol-Shooting Championship in 1939, where people asked him, "Did you come to watch?" That scene was replayed nine years later at the Olympic Games in London. When Carlos Valiente, the current world champion and Olympic favorite, spotted Takács, he asked him, "Why are you here?" Takács replied, "I'm here to learn." After Takács won the gold medal (beating the world record by 10 points), he took his place on the podium next to Valiente, who finished second. Valiente turned to him and said, "You have learned enough." When Takács won his second gold medal in Helsinki in 1952, he became the first repeat winner of the rapid-fire pistol event.

Teaching Tip

In the writing / discussion exercise, students write about a national hero. Alternately, they could write about a personal hero—a parent or grandparent, for example.

Unit 20   The Bottle

Some readers—especially young readers who were born long after the Vietnam War ended—might wonder why Hoa Van Nguyen fled his country.

Vietnam was part of French Indochina until 1954, when the French were ousted by communist forces led by Ho Chi Minh. Subsequently, the communists took control of the North, and the United States supported the South, at first economically and then militarily. The United States withdrew from Vietnam after signing a cease-fire agreement in 1973. Two years later, the North Vietnamese overran the South.

Hoa was one of an estimated 1 million South Vietnamese whom the North Vietnamese confined in "reeducation camps." When he was released in 1979, Hoa and his brother joined the throngs of Vietnamese "boat people" and fled in a small fishing boat. Eventually, they found their way to a refugee camp in Thailand, where Hoa met his future wife. Finding Mrs. Peckham's bottle was extraordinarily lucky, not only because the Peckhams were able to help the Nguyens get settled in Los Angeles (the Peckhams found them an apartment and partially furnished it) but also because the connection to the Peckhams probably shortened the time the family spent in the refugee camp. They were there two years, but it was not unusual for refugees to spend five or even ten years in a camp. Finding the bottle may also have helped Hoa psychologically. In an interview with *People* magazine, he said, "It gave me hope."

This story has a sequel. In 1990 an ESL student named Phuong, who was taking classes at the College of Marin in California, was leafing through *True Stories in the News* when he spotted Hoa Van Nguyen in the photo that accompanies "The Bottle." He exclaimed in class that he knew Hoa. They had become close friends when they were together in the "reeducation camp." After fleeing Vietnam, they had lost touch.

Phuong wrote the author of *True Stories in the News* and asked for help finding his friend, with whom he had shared "a lot of sadness and happiness." The author contacted the Vietnamese social worker at Catholic Charities who had helped the Nguyens settle in Los Angeles. The social worker put Phuong in touch with Hoa, and the two old friends arranged a reunion.

Following the reunion, Hoa and Phuong renewed their friendship in frequent visits to each other's homes. On one visit to northern California, Hoa brought along his brother (also in the photo), who ended up marrying one of Phuong's neighbors.

Teaching Tip

According to the story, Mrs. Peckham and Hoa wrote "back and forth." A writing activity called "Pen Pals in Class" ties in nicely with this unit. It is described in the teacher resource publication *Hands-on English* (Vol. II, No. 2). These are the suggested steps:

1. Students write their names on small slips of paper. The papers are put facedown on a desk. Students draw a name.

2. Students spend about 15 minutes writing a short letter to the person whose name they drew. In their letters, they first tell something about themselves and then ask two questions. (You may need to act as a scribe for students with limited writing skills.)

3. Students sign their letters and deliver them to the student whose name they drew.

4. The recipients of the letters write a reply. (Again, allow approximately 15 minutes.)

5. The replies are delivered to the original sender.

6. If the students seem to enjoy writing to in-class pen pals, the correspondence could continue in a subsequent class period.

Another possible writing activity is to ask students to imagine this: You are walking on a beach when you find a bottle. In the bottle, there is a piece of paper with a name, an address, and a message. The message is, "If you find this bottle, write to me." Write a short letter to the person who put the message in the bottle. Tell the person a little about yourself.

Unit 21 The Last Laugh

The contest was actually broader than the one presented in the story. Jodee worked for a national restaurant chain, and the contest was among the waitresses at all the chain's restaurants in a region of Florida. (All the servers at this chain are female.) First, the waitresses at each restaurant competed to see who could sell the most food and drinks during the month of May. Then the top waitresses at each restaurant entered a drawing. Jodee's name was picked. So it is conceivable that the prize for winning such a contest could be a new car.

Lawyers for the restaurant chain argued that Jodee should not be allowed to pursue her case in court. When she was hired, she had signed an employee handbook, indicating her acceptance of company policies. One policy stated that an employee with a complaint against the company had to try mediation before suing. However, the judge ruled that the company handbook was not a legal document and that Jodee had the right to sue.

Jodee was not allowed to reveal the exact terms of the settlement. It is assumed that the company, not the regional manager, paid for the new car. What model Toyota did Jodee choose? Her lawyer could not disclose the details but said that Jodee could "pick out whatever type of Toyota she wants."

Teaching Tip

Some of the students in one class that participated in field-testing this story were not familiar with the *Star Wars* movies or the character Yoda. Before the students read the story, the teacher briefly explained: "*Star Wars* were popular movies, and Yoda was in most of them. He was a teacher. People went to him when they had a problem, and he always had good ideas for them." Lack of familiarity with Yoda did not impede students' comprehension of the story, however.

The idea for the writing / discussion exercise is from the teacher resource book *Drawing Out* by Sharron Bassano and Mary Ann Christison, Alta Book Center Publishers (www.altaesl.com), 1995 (p. 53, "Work, Work, Work!"). This sequence of steps— drawing, writing, and sharing—is typical of many of the activities in *Drawing Out*. The authors state that student drawings provide a focus for oral interaction, reduce tension, and build a feeling of community spirit through shared experience. You will almost certainly discover that this activity lives up to that promise.

An alternate writing / discussion exercise is: Ask students to imagine they can go to a car dealer and pick out any car. They do not have to pay for it. What car will they choose? Ask them to draw a picture of their "dream car" and share the picture in a small group.

Unit 22 Old Friends

In 1962 the Communist Party wanted Charlie to say that the U.S. Marines had treated the Chinese badly. (The "soldiers" in the story were actually Marines.) Charlie refused, saying he'd forgotten the past. He

was convicted of suspicion of espionage and sentenced to seven years in a labor camp followed by ten years of house arrest. When his house arrest ended in 1979, Charlie decided to contact his old Marine buddies. His mother had burned his Marine possessions—including his address book—in an effort to protect him, but Charlie remembered three addresses that he had memorized 31 years earlier. He wrote three letters, and one reached its destination. When he got off the plane in the United States in 1983, four of his former buddies met him. Charlie greeted them with the words "Semper Fi," short for the Marine motto Semper Fidelis—"always faithful."

Charlie became a U.S. citizen in 2000 and an "honorary Marine" in a ceremony in 2002. In an interview with the *Chapel Hill News*, Charlie said, "I've always considered myself a Marine. Some of my old friends came for the ceremony. Some of them were in poor health, but they came anyway. They said they wouldn't miss it for the world. It's a very happy day, not only for me, but for all my good friends in the Marines."

Charlie's restaurant, which he named Tsing Tao after his native village, was a success. He retired from the restaurant business in 2007.

Teaching Tip

In the first writing / discussion exercise, students draw pictures of dishes from their native countries. These pictures could be displayed in the room and used as the basis of a lesson in which students practice ordering in a restaurant.

The story also invites a discussion of tongue twisters. Tell the students, "The American soldiers couldn't say 'Chi Hsii.' The Chinese words were too difficult for them. There are English phrases and sentences that are difficult for English-speaking people to say. These words are called 'tongue twisters.'"

Following are some simple tongue twisters for students to try:

1. She sees cheese.

2. Great gray goats

3. Mrs. Smith's Fish Sauce Shop

4. The soldier's shoulder hurts.

5. Fred fed Ted bread, and Ted fed Fred bread.

6. A big black bug bit a big black dog on his big black nose.

Students could also share tongue twisters in their native languages with the class.

Answer Key

Unit 1

VOCABULARY

2. a   3. b   4. c

REMEMBERING DETAILS

2. ~~ticket~~ / sample   6. ~~dishes~~ / salad
3. ~~orange~~ / lemon   7. ~~fine~~ / sick
4. ~~eat~~ / try   8. ~~soup~~ / soap
5. ~~bananas~~ / lemons   9. ~~coffee~~ / tea

UNDERSTANDING CAUSE AND EFFECT

2. c   3. b   4. a

UNDERSTANDING A SUMMARY

2

DISCUSSION

1. a   2. b   3. b

WRITING

In his mailbox, he found a free sample of dish soap. The dish soap had a little lemon juice in it.

    Joe looked at his bottle of soap. There was a picture of two lemons on the label. Over the lemons were the words "with Real Lemon Juice."

    Joe thought the soap was lemon juice. He put it on his salad and ate it. After he ate the salad, he felt sick. Poor Joe!

Unit 2

VOCABULARY

2. a   3. c   4. b

LOOKING FOR DETAILS

potatoes, fried vegetables, meat, dessert, sandwiches, cake; baked beans on toast, fish, vegetables

REVIEWING THE STORY

2. seat   7. woman
3. back   8. stop
4. die   9. pounds
5. diet   10. married
6. weight

UNDERSTANDING CAUSE AND EFFECT

2. d   3. a   4. b   5. e

Unit 3

VOCABULARY

2. e   3. c   4. a   5. d

REMEMBERING DETAILS

2. nursing home
3. police officers drove to Torggate Street
4. one kilometer away
5. address
6. 94 years old

UNDERSTANDING DIALOG

2. e   3. b   4. a   5. d

Unit 4

VOCABULARY

2. ready   3. can't believe it   4. delivered

UNDERSTANDING WORD GROUPS

labels, soccer, doctor

REMEMBERING DETAILS

2. ~~P.M.~~ / A.M.
3. ~~morning~~ / weekend
4. ~~schools~~ / restaurants
5. ~~write~~ / marry
6. ~~postcards~~ / letters
7. ~~70~~ / 700
8. ~~wrote~~ / delivered

UNDERSTANDING QUOTATIONS

2. d   3. b   4. a

Unit 5

VOCABULARY

2. broke into   3. stolen   4. without

UNDERSTANDING THE MAIN IDEAS

2. a   3. b   4. b   5. a

REMEMBERING DETAILS

~~truck~~ / car; ~~dirty~~ / broken; ~~back~~ / front; ~~purse~~ / wallet; ~~movie~~ / music; ~~hamburger~~ / pizza; ~~Wednesday~~ / Monday; ~~woman~~ / man

Unit 6

VOCABULARY

2. adopted   3. found out   4. exactly

UNDERSTANDING THE MAIN IDEA

1. b   2. c

LOOKING FOR DETAILS

color eyes; smile; dark, curly hair; birthday

UNDERSTANDING CAUSE AND EFFECT

2. a   3. b   4. c   5. d

Unit 7

VOCABULARY

2. c   3. a   4. b

FINDING INFORMATION
2. His farm is in Mexico.
3. His farm is close to the border.
4. Tomás went to the United States.
5. A U.S. Border Patrol officer found Tomás under a bush.
6. Tomás was alive.
7. Tomás was 15 miles from his home.

UNDERSTANDING PRONOUNS
2. f   3. e   4. b   5. a   6. d

UNDERSTANDING A SUMMARY
1

Unit 8

VOCABULARY
2. simple   3. grave   4. ground

REMEMBERING DETAILS
2. ~~Sammy~~ / Bobby
3. ~~1958~~ / 1858
4. ~~Ireland~~ / Scotland
5. ~~four~~ / fourteen
6. ~~large~~ / small
7. ~~man~~ / dog

REVIEWING THE STORY
2. fire
3. hungry
4. lonely
5. rainy
6. weather
7. years

Unit 9

VOCABULARY
2. missing
3. notice
4. coughed
5. throat

UNDERSTANDING THE MAIN IDEA
1. a   2. c

REMEMBERING DETAILS
2. ~~pie~~ / cake
3. ~~spoons~~ / coins
4. ~~breakfast~~ / dinner
5. ~~floor~~ / table
6. ~~sixth~~ / fourth
7. ~~days~~ / years
8. ~~cake~~ / coin

UNDERSTANDING A SUMMARY
2

Unit 10

VOCABULARY
2. almost
3. rent
4. got caught

UNDERSTANDING WORD GROUPS
shopping, pizza, perfectly

REVIEWING THE STORY
2. dance
3. leg
4. cast
5. bandage
6. wheelchair
7. without
8. girlfriend

UNDERSTANDING TIME RELATIONSHIPS
2. d   3. e   4. a   5. b

Unit 11

VOCABULARY
2. buried
3. terrible
4. hurried
5. dug up

REMEMBERING DETAILS
2. ~~months~~ / days
3. ~~daughter~~ / son
4. ~~wonderful~~ / terrible
5. ~~laughed~~ / screamed
6. ~~closed~~ / opened
7. ~~stomach~~ / side
8. ~~neighbor~~ / doctor
9. ~~ears~~ / lips
10. ~~year~~ / week

UNDERSTANDING TIME AND PLACE
WHEN: the next night, in 1865, at four o'clock in the morning, a week later
WHERE: in the United States, in the town cemetery, in Germany, in his bed

UNDERSTANDING QUOTATIONS
2. d   3. b   4. a

Unit 12

VOCABULARY
2. cashier
3. counter
4. lottery ticket
5. won

UNDERSTANDING WORD GROUPS
potatoes, diet, sick

REMEMBERING DETAILS
2. ~~movie~~ / lottery
3. ~~floor~~ / counter
4. ~~money~~ / tickets
5. ~~$5~~ / $50,000
6. ~~anger~~ / shock
7. ~~uncle~~ / mother
8. ~~friendly~~ / honest

UNDERSTANDING CAUSE AND EFFECT
2. d   3. a   4. b

Unit 13

VOCABULARY
2. a   3. b   4. a

UNDERSTANDING THE MAIN IDEAS
2. b   3. b   4. b   5. a   6. a

UNDERSTANDING A SUMMARY
1

DISCUSSION / WRITING
A.
2. shrimp and small fish
3. about 1,400 kilograms (3,080 pounds)
4. for 12 months
5. about 907 kilograms (2,000 pounds)
6. milk from its mother
B.
2. They eat shrimp and small fish.
3. It eats about 1,400 kilograms (3,080 pounds) of food every day.

4. She is pregnant for 12 months.
5. It weighs about 907 kilograms (2,000 pounds).
6. It drinks milk from its mother.

Unit 14

VOCABULARY
2. a   3. a   4. b

FINDING INFORMATION
2. b, c   3. a, b   4. a, c   5. b, c

MAKING CONNECTIONS
2. a   3. d   4. c

REMEMBERING DETAILS
2. ~~peace~~ / freedom   4. ~~daughters~~ / sons
3. ~~California~~ / Florida   5. ~~ten~~ / two

Unit 15

VOCABULARY
2. trouble   3. shouted   4. plenty

REMEMBERING DETAILS
~~July~~ / June; ~~family~~ / friends; ~~Peru~~ / Colombia;
~~rainstorm~~ / snowstorm; ~~pocket~~ / backpack; ~~radio~~ / cell
phone; ~~hours~~ / minutes; ~~man~~ / woman; ~~ski~~ / rescue

UNDERSTANDING DIALOG
lost, minutes, help, Stay

FINDING MORE INFORMATION
2. a   3. e   4. b   5. d

Unit 16

VOCABULARY
2. a   3. b   4. a

FINDING INFORMATION
2. a, b   3. b, c   4. b, c   5. b, c

UNDERSTANDING CAUSE AND EFFECT
2. d   3. a   4. c

LOOKING FOR DETAILS
his job, the weather, the food, the water
American sports, American food

Unit 17

VOCABULARY
2. wedding   4. changed his mind
3. guests

UNDERSTANDING THE MAIN IDEAS
2. c   3. c   4. a

UNDERSTANDING QUOTATIONS
2. c   3. d   4. a

Unit 18

VOCABULARY
2. b   3. a   4. a

FINDING INFORMATION
2. Jimmy and his father were playing on a Chicago
   beach.
3. Jimmy ran onto the ice.
4. The ice broke.
5. Firefighters pulled Jimmy out of the water.
6. Jimmy was in the water for over twenty minutes.

UNDERSTANDING CAUSE AND EFFECT
2. e   3. a   4. b   5. c

UNDERSTANDING WORD GROUPS
pilot, nervous, garden

Unit 19

VOCABULARY
2. army   5. medal
3. exploded   6. hero
4. happened

UNDERSTANDING WORD GROUPS
letter, school, excited

FINDING INFORMATION
2. eight years
3. to the Olympics
4. the Hungarian team
5. the gold medal in pistol shooting
6. In 1952

UNDERSTANDING SEQUENCE
1939   He won the Hungarian National Pistol-Shooting
          Competition.
1940–1948   He practiced for the Olympics.
1948   He won his first Olympic gold medal.
1952   He won his second Olympic gold medal.

Unit 20

VOCABULARY
2. floating   3. tears

FINDING INFORMATION
2. b, c   3. a, c   4. a, b   5. a, c   6. a, b

UNDERSTANDING A SUMMARY
2

UNDERSTANDING WORD GROUPS
Los Angeles, at the airport, boss

Unit 21

VOCABULARY
2. d   3. e   4. a   5. c

REVIEWING THE STORY

2. contest   5. movies
3. win   6. judge
4. hard

FINDING MORE INFORMATION

2. a   3. b   4. e   5. c

Unit 22

VOCABULARY

2. village   3. over   4. traded

REMEMBERING DETAILS

2. ~~doctors~~ / soldiers
3. ~~I~~ / II
4. ~~fruit~~ / eggs
5. ~~Spanish~~ / English
6. ~~days~~ / years
7. ~~England~~ / the United States
8. ~~never~~ / often

UNDERSTANDING CAUSE AND EFFECT

2. a   3. d   4. c

UNDERSTANDING A SUMMARY

1

Acknowledgments

I wish to thank:

▶ the many teachers who have e-mailed me, written me, or sought me out at TESOL conventions to tell me about their experiences with the *True Stories* books. Your feedback helps me assess how the stories and exercises are working outside the small sphere of my own classroom. Your suggestions are always very welcome;

▶ the teachers who suggested ways to improve *True Stories in the News* for this third edition and the program directors who put me in touch with those teachers. In particular, I wish to acknowledge:

▶ Carol Hornreich, Henriette VanWoerkom, Lauren Brown, and Diane Johnston, New Haven (CT) Adult Education Program; Greg Keech, Kevin Cross, Terrie Pon, and Robert Schuricht, San Francisco (CA) City College; David Red, Suellen Stover, Susanne Stahovec, John Carlson, Fairfax County (VA) Adult Education; Kathi Hart, IEP, Denver (CO) University; Anjie Martin, Whitewater (WI) Community Education; Peggy Miles, Santa Cruz (CA) Adult School; Cheryl Nuwash, Texas Intensive English Program, Austin, TX; Tiia Reinwald, NE Family Reader Development Program, YMCA, Philadelphia, PA; David Tapia, English Language Learner Services, Bakersfield (CA) City Schools; Jon Tegnell, Warabi High School, Saitama, Japan; Abbie Tom, Durham (NC) Technical College;

▶ my students at the Whitewater (WI) Community Education Adult ESL Program, who gave me their honest opinions of the stories and exercises;

▶ Sharron Bassano, who lent her expertise in collaborative learning strategies to improve the discussion exercises. (The discussion exercises for Units 16 and 21 are her ideas);

▶ Robert Ruvo, production editor, and Karen Davy, development editor, whose skilled and experienced hands guided this book through its final stages;

▶ Kathy Olson, who demonstrated several of the post-reading activities suggested in the To the Teacher section at TESOL 2007 (in a presentation titled "Repetition: Multiple Activities Using One Reading Selection");

▶ Penny Ur and Andrew Wright, who describe the "Disappearing Summary" activity suggested in the To the Teacher section in their teacher resource book *Five-Minute Activities* (Cambridge University Press, 1992) and who in turn credit the activity to Michael Buckby;

▶ Jill DeGrange, who suggested the discussion exercise in Unit 1;

▶ Mark Lewis and Hsiao Shu-lun at the UPI office in Taipei, Taiwan, who verified the story "The Love Letters";

▶ Yuan Guey Chiou, who wrote the letter in the photograph in Unit 4;

▶ Robert Seger, Director of the Clinton Public Library in Iowa, who steered me to people who knew about Max Hoffman;

▶ William Rolston, who sent a photo of Max Hoffman, and Edward Ridyard, who sent Max Hoffman's autobiography;

▶ Tan Ho, who sent the story about the whale to my colleague Katherine Conover, who in turn sent the story to me;

▶ adult learner K-C Kim, who provided the writing example in Unit 15;

▶ Elvira Vida, media manager at the Hungarian National Tourist Office, who helped me find the photo of Olympic champion Károly Takács;

▶ Louise Austin, Whitewater (WI) Community Education, who developed the "international restaurant" activity suggested in Unit 22;

▶ Dorothy Peckham and Chi Hsii Tsui (Charlie Two Shoes), the protagonists in two of the stories, who gave me information not found in news sources. Thank you for sharing that information with me and with the readers of this book.